Smithfield and the parish of St Paul

Maynooth Studies in Local History

SERIES EDITOR Raymond Gillespie

This is one of six short books published in the Maynooth Studies in Local History series in 2005. Like their predecessors they are, in the main, drawn from theses presented for the MA course in local history at NUI Maynooth. Also, like their predecessors, they range widely over the local experience in the Irish past. That local experience is presented in the context of the complex social and political world of which it is part, from the great houses of Armagh to the rural housing of Leitrim and from the property developers of eighteenth-century Dublin to those who rioted on the streets of the capital. The local experience cannot be a simple chronicling of events relating to an area within administrative or geographically-determined boundaries since understanding the local world presents much more complex challenges for the historian. It is an investigation of the socially diverse worlds of poor and rich. It explores the lives of those who joined the British army in the First World War as well as those who, on principle, chose not to do so. Reconstructing such diverse local worlds relies on understanding what the people of the different communities that made up the localities of Ireland had in common and what drove them apart. Understanding the assumptions, often unspoken, around which these local societies operated is the key to recreating the world of the Irish past and gaining insight into how the people who inhabited those worlds lived their daily lives. As such, studies such as those presented in these short books, together with their predecessors, are at the forefront of Irish historical research and represent some of the most innovative and exciting work being undertaken in Irish history today. They also provide models that others can follow and adapt in their own studies of the Irish past. In such ways can we better understand the regional diversity of Ireland and the social and cultural basis of that diversity. If these books also convey something of the vibrancy and excitement of the world of Irish local history today they will have achieved at least some of their purpose.

Maynooth Studies in Local History: Number 63

Smithfield and the parish of St Paul, Dublin, 1698–1750

Brendan Twomey

FOUR COURTS PRESS

Set in 10pt on 12pt Bembo by
Carrigboy Typesetting Services, County Cork for
FOUR COURTS PRESS LTD
7 Malpas Street, Dublin 8, Ireland
e-mail: info@four-courts-press.ie
http://www.four-courts-press.ie
and in North America for
FOUR COURTS PRESS
c/o ISBS, 920 N.E. 58th Avenue, Suite 300, Portland, OR 97213.

ISBN 1–85182–895–8

Printed in Ireland by
ßetaprint Ltd, Dublin

Contents

Acknowledgments

I wish to acknowledge the support and assistance that was provided to me by many people in the preparation of this book. Firstly, I wish to express my thanks to the archivists and librarians in the various institutions that house the primary source material that I consulted. In particular I would like to thank Dr Raymond Refaussé and Dr Susan Hood in the RCB Library, Leslie Whiteside archivist of King's Hospital and Aideen Ireland in the National Archives of Ireland. Their help and guidance was much appreciated. A special thanks is also due to the archivists, librarians and staff in the National Library of Ireland, Colette Eliston in the Royal Society of Antiquaries of Ireland, Penny Woods of the Russell Library in National University of Ireland Maynooth, the staff of the Department of Early Printed Books in Trinity College Dublin and of the National Archives in Kew and Dr Maire Kennedy in the Dublin City Library and Archive in Pearse Street all of whom were ever-helpful in finding the requested material.

Secondly I wish to thank members of the Department of Modern History in the National University of Ireland Maynooth especially my supervisor Prof. Jacqueline Hill for her guidance and encouragement and my second-year course leader Dr Terence Dooley. I would like to express a special thanks to the first-year course leader Prof. Raymond Gillespie for his overall support and specifically for his insights into the arcane workings of the parish vestry in eighteenth-century Ireland. I would also like to express my thanks to Dr Toby Barnard for the advice and ideas given on our chance encounters in the RCB library.

Finally I would like to express my sincere thanks to my wife Valerie for her understanding and support while this book was being prepared, and for her forbearance at not seeing the normal quota of 'jobs' being achieved during that time.

Introduction

Eighteenth-century Ireland has been referred to as the era of the Protestant Ascendancy although this specific term only came into common usage in the last decades of the century at a point when the political contrivance that it purported to describe was coming to an end.[1] There is no doubt that the concept of a confessional qualification for political rights and privileges at both a local and national level was a feature of the Irish polity throughout the 18th century.[2] While this system of government was far from uncommon in 18th century Europe, a distinctive feature of the Irish confessional state was that political rights and power were confined to a religious minority of perhaps no more than one tenth of the population of the entire island.[3] The city of Dublin was however, an exception to this national denominational ratio. In the last decades of the 17th century and the early decades of the 18th century Dublin was a Protestant city. Of an estimated population of circa 70,000 in 1710 about 40,000, or nearly 60 per cent, were Protestant. By mid-century there were approximately 3,000 freemen in Dublin. These freemen belonged to the various trade-based guilds, most were members of the established church – the Church of Ireland – and each had a vote in the Dublin constituency of the Irish parliament.[4] The Protestant citizenry of Dublin therefore included not only the well-known figures, who populate the political and cultural history of the period, it also included the Protestant freemen most of whose names we know, but the detail of whose lives and business and civic activities are not particularly well known.[5]

This book analyses the property, parochial and civic activities of one group within this 18th-century Dublin urban Protestant community. By describing some of the detailed activities of this group we can reconstruct aspects of the civic and business life of Protestant Dublin in this period. The focus is on the local Protestant community leadership in the Smithfield area in the suburb of Oxmantown and in the newly established parish of St Paul.[6] The individuals within this group knew one another intimately. They were connected by layers of relationships across their parochial, civic, business and family affairs. The analysis is confined to the period 1698 to 1750 and to the area covered by, and the people who feature in, the 237 pages and the 53 years covered by the first vestry minute book of the parish of St Paul.[7] This book uses five principal primary written historical sources to trace the lives and actions of this local elite viz. the vestry minute book and the parish registers of the parish of St Paul, the memorials in the

Registry of Deeds of the leases and mortgages of William Hendrick, local property developer member of the city assembly and vestryman of St Paul's parish, the minute and account books of the Blue Coat School, the building estimates and receipts for the repair of Sir Robert Echlin's house in Queen Street in 1745–7 and the *Calendar of the ancient records of Dublin*.[8] These sources are formal in tone and content and they therefore provide little insight into individual mentalities. We still await the discovery for Dublin of an autobiography or cache of letters to rival that of a Pole Cosby or a Bishop Synge. Such a source would enable historians to marry the actions recorded in the formal civic, ecclesiastical and business records with more intimate indications of personal thoughts and beliefs as outlined in more personal documents.[9] Nevertheless, when these contemporary records are read with a focus on tracing the lives and actions of a small number of specific individuals, in a narrow time-span, and in a restricted geographic space, they can shed light not only on individual transactions but also on patterns of family, business, political and cultural connections in early 18th-century Protestant Dublin. The impacts on this local elite of other trends in 18th-century Irish society, such as the emerging print culture and the expanding public sphere, the rapidly changing political culture and, perhaps most critically, the penal laws are not considered in this book.

This book is organised into three chapters. Chapter one describes aspects of the evolving morphology of the Smithfield St Paul's area in the late 17th and early 18th centuries. There is a particular focus on the business activities of William Hendrick a local property developer in the Smithfield St Paul's area. Chapter two examines the role of and activity of the parish vestry of the newly established parish of St Paul in the first decades of the 18th century. It focuses in particular on the construction of and the maintenance of the fabric of the parish church, on some aspects of the financial management of the parish and also on the civic role of the parish vestry in managing the local parish watch and in making returns to the lord mayor on the standards of paving in the neighbourhood. Chapter three gives brief biographies of four members of the parish vestry in this period – Bruen Worthington, Henry Westenra, Richard Tighe and William Hendrick – and also of the first three rectors of the parish of St Paul – Ezekiel Burridge, Charles Carr and Duke Tyrrell. Chapter five draws some brief conclusions from the evidence adduced in this book. Some of these themes and sources have been explored by other authors in particular the PhD theses of Nuala Burke and Rowena Dudley, the published vestry minutes edited by Raymond Gillespie and the extensive source-based work of Toby Barnard.[10]

From the middle of the 17th century Dublin experienced very rapid extramural growth. New suburban areas, with a mixture of residential, commercial and industrial activities, were developed all around the old city walls. In the early decades of the 18th-century the Smithfield St Paul's area was one of the most vibrant and rapidly growing of these suburbs. The legacy of the men who were involved in managing this growth is still with us today in some fragmentary remains of the 18th century building fabric, in the street layout and in many of the street names in the area. When reviewing their actions and the issues that they had to address the modern reader will recognize patterns that are repeated in our time and in any city that is experiencing rapid development. There is evidence of the operation of golden circles or coteries of influence in early 18th-century Dublin, of conflicting patterns of land use, of planning, legal and administrative disputes and of dissatisfaction at the level of service provision by the civic authorities. There is also evidence of the burden that was placed on a small number of voluntary activists, drawn exclusively from a narrow pool of adherents to the state religion, but nonetheless called on to act for and represent the interests of the wider community.

1. The construction of the Smithfield St Paul's area

In many ways the evolution of the built environment of the Smithfield area between the restoration and the middle of the 18th century is a case study of urban development in Dublin in this period. In the last decades of the 17th century and the early decades of the 18th century Dublin grew rapidly and its suburbs spread far beyond the confining walls of the medieval city. The development model of those who managed and administered this growth was heavily influenced by trends both in London and elsewhere in Europe. The use of the names Smithfield and Haymarket in Dublin in the 1660s (copied from earlier developments in London) is but one modest example of this external influence.[1] Most of the new suburban houses built in this period were multi-storey Dutch Billy town houses of uniform pattern with a narrow street frontage, a basement, a back yard (or backside as referred to in contemporary leases), external latrines, wells, coach houses and stables which were usually accessed through a subsidiary roadway. The growth in building activity in the city in this period spurred innovation in a number of other sectors including the development of increasingly sophis-ticated mortgage and fire insurance markets.[2] Dublin corporation was the leading agency of local government in Dublin throughout the 18th century. The primary decision making body of the corporation was the city assembly the meetings of which were concerned with the management of the city's land and other assets, provision of civic services and the overall financial and administrative management of the city.[3] From the 1660s onwards significant sections of the city's extensive land bank were alienated, by means of long leases, to some of the city's leading merchants for the development of new suburban housing. The first of these land grants involved the allocation of a large number of building lots in Oxmantown and St Stephen's Green in the 1660s.[4]

As well as encouraging the expansion of the city the civic authorities were also intimately involved in improving its physical environment through the provision of lighting, paving, fire fighting, piped-water and other services. Policing and security was also an abiding concern of the civic authorities in early 18th-century Dublin and from 1716 the parish watch system was the subject of successive waves of reform aimed at increasing its overall effectiveness.[5] The triennial Riding the Franchises, by the lord mayor, aldermen, assembly members and representatives of the guilds, was one of

1 View of the north bank of the Liffey from Bloody Bridge – Francis Place 1698 (Courtesy of the national Gallery of Ireland). This drawing shows the north bank of the river after the construction of the Bowling Green and some enquaying of the north bank. It pre-dates the building of the Royal Barracks, the Gravel Walk Slip and the streets built by William Hendrick in the 1720s.

the rituals used by the corporation to assert and delineate the area of its authority. Part of the boundary of St Michan's parish (later the boundary for St Paul's parish) was described colourfully in the riding of the franchises in 1603;

> From thence they make their way to Bow-bridge, and pass under the middle arch of the said bridge, and then into the hospital fields, over the old Deer-park wall, near the old Slaughter-house. From thence through the Hospital-fields, and across the Liffey-strand to a round stone by the Deer-park wall. From thence they pass over the Deer-park wall, and through a part of the park to a corner of the wall near a dog-kennel, on the north-side thereof. From thence over the said wall northward, and passed along the same to the first half round or rising on the said wall. Thence they proceed eastward through Mr Bartholomew's fields, and several gardens to Stoneybatter, on the south end of Mr Addisons' house, and from thence through a house at which hangs a sign of the Half-moon, on the east side of Stoneybatter, and through the gardens to Colonel Stanley's house, and through the said house to Grange-Gorman-lane. From thence by the south end of the Half-moon, on the east side of Grange-Gorman-lane and through the gardens into Finglass-road, and from thence northward to the Broad-Stone:[6]

Smithfield was one of the earliest of the new extramural suburbs to be built in Dublin. In 1665 over 90 building plots, on the corporation owned land in Oxmantown, were allocated by the drawing of lots. The initial intention seems to have been to create a high-status suburb, however, despite some initial indications of success, Smithfield failed to retain its early social lead over the rival development in St Stephen's Green.[7] The city assembly also allocated a significant plot to the duke of Ormond in this period, however, the duke did not utilise the site and some 40 years later it became the site of the Royal Barracks. One possible reason for the decline of the area was the conflict between high-status housing developments and other land uses such as industry and horse and cattle markets. Local property owners were not unaware of this dilemma, for example in 1744 Welbore Ellis inserted a clause in a lease that forbade residents to 'carry on the business of tallow chandler, dyer or other offensive business'.[8] By then however, it was probably too late for the Smithfield area to retain any pretensions to high social status and, having declined in status throughout the 18th century, the area became, in the 19th century, a centre for industry, cattle and hay markets, warehousing and working-class housing. By the end of the 20th century the area was experiencing many of the symptoms associated with urban decay.[9] However, in the past ten years significant redeveloped has taken place in the area including the refurbishment of the open ground of Smithfield and the construction of a major apartment and commercial development on the site of the 1665 development on the west side of Smithfield and the east side of Queen Street.[10]

Building work apparently started immediately on the allocated building plots in Smithfield and, as early as August 1666, the duke of Ormond petitioned the city assembly to allow St Stephen's Green to be used for military exercises due to the fact of 'the many buildings lately made on Oxmantowne Greene … have taken up soe much roome there that his majesties horse and foote guards and the citty militia have not conveniency to exercise as formerly'.[11] This petition would seem to reinforce the social inferiority of St Stephen's Green in this early period when St Stephens was also used as the site of the principal gallows in the city. In 1664 the initial high social status of the Smithfield area was confirmed when, even before the granting of the building plots, the city assembly granted Alderman Richard Tighe an extensive strip of ground to construct a Bowling Green and 'a convenient house on some part of the said ground for the accommodation of gentlemen and others which shall resort to the said Greene'. However, Tighe was only given title to the ground for the Bowling Green on the condition that he would have to pay a sizeable fine of £100 per annum if the ground was put to any other use.[12] The city authorities arranged for a path to be built at the southern end of the Bowling Green and for it to be shaded with elms and sycamores.[13] This path became known as Gravel Walk, the name shown in the Rocque map of 1756, and which name has recently been recalled by the naming of a new apartment block on Blackhall Place and Hendrick Street as Gravel Walk Court. In 1699 John Dunton described the Bowling Green as 'perhaps the finest in Europe' and 'the only thing that Dublin exceeds or equals London'.[14] In 1665 the writer of a letter in the *Calendar of state papers relating to Ireland* noted that 'Alderman Tye's new Bowling Green (played upon so airy a ground) so fans the nobility of both sexes every day that no immoderate heat offends them or putrifies their blood.'[15] The Bowling

Green was a feature of the landscape of Oxmantown for 60 years until permission to develop the site was given by the city assembly to Richard Tighe's grandson in 1724. The Bowling Green was still depicted as an open space on Brooking's map of 1728 however, in the Rocque map of 1756 while it was still an open space, it had been significantly reduced in size by the encroachment of new streets.[16]

Following the initial land grants the consolidation of the river shoreline was proceeded with in the last decades of the seventeenth century by means of the grant of river frontage to William Ellis in 1682 and the subsequent construction of quays and bridges.[17] Ellis's grant stretched all the way along the river tidal flats from close to the site of the old bridge up-stream to the Phoenix Park gate. The complex conditions imposed on Ellis by the city assembly included a stipulation that he build a quay, 36 feet wide and that it should completed within the first seven years of the lease on pain of a doubling of the rent to the city. Ellis's freedom to develop was also restricted in that development between the Bowling Green and the river was subject to Tighe's consent. Ellis was also obliged to build a new stone bridge at Queen Street and to replace the existing wooden bridge at Bloody Bridge – although a grant of £700 from city taxation was made available to him for this project. Ellis began by concentrating his efforts on what is now Arran Quay, building the quay wall, and reclaiming the land behind it. The engineering works provided a supply of water-rolled cobbles that were used in the construction of the plot walls and latrines in Smithfield and Queen Street.[18] Despite extensive new building in the area from 1665 onward Oxmantown Green remained a prominent feature of the area for many decades. In 1728 the guild of St Mary (carpenters) asked for permission to construct some houses for poor brethren and sisters on a site on the green. The permission was granted for this and 'no other purpose' and the permission also stipulated that the development was to have no direct entrance to the green and that no sewers were to be built onto the green.[19] This development proceeded and a building surrounded by a wall with access only to Arbour Hill and entitled 'Carpenters Widdow House' was shown on Rocque's map of 1756. The imposition of a condition of not having direct access to the green or of interfering with its environment was also contained in several other city land grants of the period. However, in the long run the efforts to preserve Oxmantown Green as an open space were unsuccessful. The lack of attention paid by Dublin corporation to the maintenance of the paving in front of the green, as evidenced by the paving returns of St Paul's parish from the 1730s, may be evidence of a lack of a real commitment by the civic authorities to the long term preservation of the green. The Blue Coat School relocated to a site on the green in 1780s and, while, the section of the green between the new school and the Carpenters Widow House was still open ground in 1821, it had been completely built on by 1876.[20]

The redevelopment of Smithfield in recent years has allowed archaeologists to carry out excavations on parts of the original 1665 development. In 2002 sections of the site of plot numbers 1–24 from the original land grant were excavated by Franc Myles of Margaret Gowan and Co.[21] The excavations uncovered evidence of burials (possibly from executions) on the eastern side of the site prior to the 1665 development. The excavation of the mid-17th century development revealed evidence of foundations of Dutch billys, garden features, a glass works, back yard latrines and wells and numerous taverns. The building material used in the construction of houses was most likely to have been the locally-made bricks that are still visible on surviving 18th-century buildings in Dublin. The roofing material on these early buildings was likely to have been of red earthenware tiles. The archaeological record would seem to indicate that from the start of the 18th century the social status of the area declined – at least on the Smithfield side of the development. In many cases there were indications that suggest the presence of an inn or a tavern on many plots on the Smithfield frontage for example in 1730 a John Connor held the sub-lease of the White Swan in Plot 3 from Allen Maddison.[22] On the Smithfield side of the site the original plots were rapidly subdivided and the archaeological evidence indicates that there was a break in the origin and quality of the pottery recovered from the deposits either side of the first quarter of the eighteenth century. There is also evidence that industries had established themselves, primarily in the back yards of the Smithfield plots, during the same period. As early as 1675, John Odacio Formica had opened the first lead glasshouse in Dublin within Plot 1 on the Haymarket frontage.[23] While the glasshouse itself was not recovered during the excavation, significant amounts of glasshouse waste was recovered, some of it from a latrine to the rear of the plot. A full examination of the artifactual assemblages from the pits and latrines to the rear of these premises will throw further light on the activities carried on within the individual businesses. The archaeological and map evidence would however support the view that the Queen Street side of the development was occupied at this time by larger more high-status buildings with open back gardens, including formal water and other features, rather than a proliferation of sub-plots and small buildings as on the Smithfield side.

In the 1720s William Hendrick was perhaps the most important property developer in the Smithfield area. The details of some of his property and financial transactions can be traced through the memorials of leases, assignments and mortgages recorded in the Registry of Deeds and also from surviving original deeds in the National Archives of Ireland and the National Library of Ireland. William Hendrick's property development activities were concentrated in the area bounded on the east by the original 1665 development on Smithfield Queen Street, on the north by North King Street and St Paul's church and churchyard, on the south by the river Liffey,

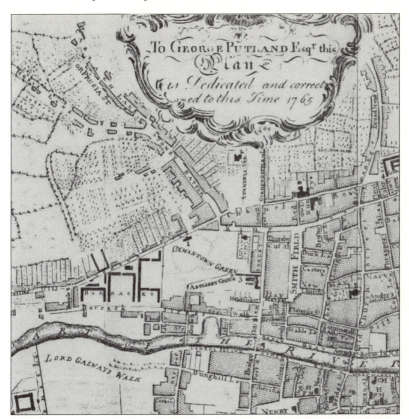

2 Rocque map of the Smithfield St Paul's area, 1765. By this time most of the streets developed by William Hendrick have been completed. Oxmantown green and the remains of the Bowling Green were however still open spaces. The Gravel Walk Slip is clearly visible to the south of Barrack Street.

from Arran Quay westwards, and to the west by the Royal Barracks. While the Hendrick family did not attain the wealth and status achieved by some other urban families in the Smithfield St Paul's area, such as the Tighes, the Putlands[24] or by Joseph Deamer[25] they were a successful business family who were involved in business and civic activities in the city over several generations. For example John Hendrick, William Hendrick's grandfather, a brewer in Islandbridge, was one of the city sheriffs in 1703.[26] Members of the Hendrick family married into the Wolfe Aylmer family at Kerdifstown near Naas and were landlords there until after the first-world-war.[27]

The value of the Registry of Deeds as a source of social, economic and morphological history has long been underestimated. The registry was established in 1708 and in many ways it was designed to supplement the penal laws. The evolution of the Irish registry meant that the records constitute 'a veritable kaleidoscope, of the wide range of contemporary transactions.' and they contain 'far more detail than was demanded by law'. The individual records in the registry usually consist of a complete copy or a fairly full abstract of a document containing all of the pertinent detail'.[28] The earliest evidence of William Hendrick's acquisition of property in the Smithfield area that has come to light is a lease between John Ellis and William Hendrick dated April 1718 for a large site fronting on to Arran Quay.[29] The complex terms set in this lease were not untypical of the terms of many of the property leases of this period. While the Ellis lease was for a long period of 120 years, immediate building was encouraged by the granting of only one year free of ground rent. The relevant clause stated that 'For the first year of the said term of one hundred and twenty years one shilling sterling and for the residue and the remainder of the said term the clear yearly rent or sum of thirty eight pounds sterling'. Rapid development was also encouraged by a stipulation that, if buildings were not erected within two years, Hendrick was required to pay six guineas per foot until the houses were erected. The inclusion of terms to encourage early development was not an usual feature of leases of the this period. For example, an advertisement in the *Dublin Gazette* of March 1710 noted that 'good encouragement will be given to tenants'.[30] The lease defined the means of payment as 'lawful money of Great Britain' and also stipulated the dates for payment as 'half yearly during the said term in even and equal parts that is to say on the first day of November and on the first day of May every year without any manner of deduction'. The term 'deduction' meant that the payment to the lessor was to be free of all property based taxes. In a later lease in 1725 William Hendrick imposed a similar condition and in it he defined some of the possible deductions that were excluded as 'all manner of taxes subsidies assessments chimney or hearth money church parish and ministers dues poorhouse or workhouse money lamp money watch money and all other taxes charges impositions and payments whatsoever charged or to be charged on the said demised premises or any part thereof during the said term'.[31] The 1718 Ellis deed also obliged William Hendrick to build to an acceptable standard when it stated that 'the said William Hendrick shall and will at his and their own proper costs and charges within the space of two years from the date of these present erect and build or cause to be erected and built one or more ... [ms illegible] dwelling houses ... of stone or brick ... slated sufficient to pay and answer the said rent of thirty eight pounds per ann[um]'.[32]

Having secured the large site on Arran Quay Hendrick set about acquiring and developing further holdings in the area. However, in the well-connected business community of Dublin of the early 1720s his plans may have been common knowledge and, as in any period of building or land speculation, they may not have met with universal approval. In January 1724 the city assembly passed a resolution which noted that:

> Certain of the commons, setting forth to the said city assembly their being apprehensive that Mr William Hendrick intends to build on the strand, opposite the Bowling Green, in Oxmantown, and to fill up the ground thereto adjoining, which will be a great prejudice to the city, and a public inconvenience, and therefore prayed that whensoever the said Mr Hendrick or any other person whatsoever attempts to put any such design in execution, or to lay any dirt between the two bridges, a speedy stop be put thereto by the Lord Mayor for the time being, and that the city indemnify his Lordship for so doing: whereupon it is granted and allowed.[33]

However, only nine months later the city assembly approved Richard Tighe's (grandson of the original lessee Alderman Richard Tighe) plans to lease the Bowling Green for development. One possible explanation for the January resolution is that it was a stratagem by the city assembly to force Tighe and Hendrick to reveal their plans and therefore to seek the necessary approval on terms more acceptable to the city assembly and in particular to force the developers to include the construction of the Gravel Walk Slip in their plans.[34] The committee examining the issue reported that 'alderman Tighe was at a considerable expense in making and finishing the said Bowling Green, and do believe that the same is not of any considerable advantage to the petitioner by reason of the other Bowling Greens which seem to be mostly resorted to for that use.'[35] The city assembly released Tighe from the fine for any change of use that had been inserted in the original lease and offered a new lease provided 'that the petitioner, at his expense, procure from Mr Hendrick two hundred feet of ground in breadth adjoining the ground lately taken in near Bloody Bridge by said Hendrick, to be left open for a watering place in lieu of the fifteen feet intended for the same use near Queen street and mentioned in the city lease to Mr Ellis'. This term implied that by this time Hendrick had secured further sites on the river although there does not appear to be a record of them in the Registry of Deeds. The construction of the slip involved inserting a breach in the quay wall. The slip was used for many years as a loading point for wood for the water pipes for the city which were stored in the city pipe yard located behind the slip in Barrack Street as shown on many contemporary maps. While the watering place was not shown on the Brooking's map of 1728 it was shown on the Rocque map of 1756 when it was described as the Gravel Walk Slip.

Having secured the requisite permission Richard Tighe leased the Bowling Green to a John Hendrick who sub-leased to William Hendrick.[36] A new street, called Hendrick Street, was laid out on the site of the Gravel

Walk leading from Queen Street to the old banqueting house and the rest of
the ground was laid out for building.[37] Despite the fact that Tighe and
Hendrick were well connected and influential members of the city business
and civic elite this affair shows that the city assembly was able to exercise
sufficient independence to secure the provision of a piece of infrastructure
for the broader common good at no cost to the city ratepayers. The deed
giving Tighe the 200 feet of ground near bloody bridge described Tighe as
'Honable. Rich. Tighe Esq. one of his Ma:ties Most Honable Privy Council
in the Kingdom of Ireland' and the purpose was stated as 'the same for ever
thereafter to be left open for a watering place which the said William Hendrick
as assignee of William Ellis was or were by lease from the Lord Mayor Sherriffs
commons and citizens of the city of Dublin obliged to leave open near
Queen's Street'. The term was for 94 years and it was to be held 'in trust for
the aforesaid with rent in pepper corn money'.[38] The prohibition of building
south of Gravel Walk was also cancelled in 1724. This ground was in a lease
from William Ellis to Mary Palliser widow of William Palliser, late archbishop
of Cashel and part of it was later sub-leased to William Hendrick and part
by John Murphy a timber merchant.[39]

Following the acquisition of these tracts of land Hendrick was in a
position to build new houses. The questions that now need to be considered
include – who built these houses, how much did they cost, how were the
site acquisition and construction costs financed and who bought and or
rented them once they were built. McKellar's analysis of this process for the
London building sector at this time concluded that the building sector had a
complex structure and in particular that it was dependent on the provision
of significant sums of mortgage-based finance. She also shows that it required
inputs from numerous parties ranging from land and property speculators, to
master builders and independent tradesmen. She concluded that, excluding
major aristocratic residences, house prices in London in this period were of
the order of £100 to £500.[40] Swift, both through his own extensive personal
financial dealings and through his involvement as a governor of Blue Coat
School, was familiar with the business practices of the Dublin property
market and also with many of the individuals involved in the speculative
property development business in the Smithfield St Paul's area. He asserted
that much actual construction was organised by guild members or by com-
binations of tradesmen such as masons, carpenters and glaziers and he
castigated the practice on a number of occasions in the 1720s. For example
in 1724, in *The truth of some maxims in state and government examined with
reference to Ireland* he stated that:

> The mason, the bricklayer, the carpenter, the slater, and the glazier,
> take a lot of ground, club to build one or more houses, unite their
> credit, their stock, and their money: and when the work is finished, sell

3 Modern Hendrick Street. The corner building on Hendrick Street and Queen
Street is the only remaining piece of eighteenth-century fabric left in Hendrick
Street. The Gravel Walk Court apartment complex is visible in the background on
the right hand side of the Hendrick Street. There were Dutch hilly houses on
Hendrick Street as late as the 1960s.

it to the best advantage they can. But, as it often happens, and more
every day, that their fund will not answer half their design, they are
forced to undersell it at the first story, and are all reduced to beggary.
Insomuch, that I know a certain fanatic brewer, who is reported to
have some hundreds of houses in this town, is said to have purchased
the greater part of them at half value from ruined undertakers: hath
intelligence of all new houses where the finishing is at a stand, takes
advantage of ready money, gets fifty per cent, at least for his bargain.[41]

As always when reading Swift one must make allowance for the inevitable
satiric tone and exaggeration. However, in the 1720s Swift was fully engaged
in a public debate on the causes of Ireland's poverty and lack of economic
development and it is likely that he was articulating some of the perceptions
of the political class at that time on aspects of the speculative building trade
in Dublin. The houses built by William Hendrick in the Queen Street area
set a standard for the neighbourhood, which he then imposed on new
developments through his building leases. In the lease to Hoffman of 1725 a
clause stated that 'all such houses as shall be built or erected on the said
demise premises shall be in all respects of equal height, storeys and orna-
ments to the houses now finishing fronting Queen Street'. The original deed
for this transaction was reused at its initial expiry in 1815, and it was noted

on the rear of the deed 'Mem. 6 Apr 1816 The leases comprised within are vested for seven years in Robert Maddock Esq. of 25 Kildare St deriving under Helsham. There are 6 houses thereon viz. 74, 75, 76, 77 Queens St. and 40, 41 Tighe Street.'[42]

A primary source that has recently come into the author's possession gives considerable insight into the complex organisation of the Dublin building trade in the 1740s. The 13 documents in the file comprise the building tradesmen's statements and receipts associated with the work carried out for Sir Robert Echlin on Mrs Bolton's house in Queen Street.[43] In 1741 Sir Robert Echlin was in negotiation with Archbishop Bolton of Cashel for the rent of a house in Queen Street. An extract of a letter from the bishop described various fixtures and fittings in the house which the bishop wished to leave in the house and which he valued at £200 and because of which he was not prepared to reduce the proposed rental level. This form of trade-off arrangement was not uncommon in early eighteenth-century leases for example in 1710 a rental advertisement in the *Dublin Gazette* noted that a house 'is to be lett : Furnish'd or unfurnish'd, with, or without a stable and coach house:[44] Sometime after 1741 Sir Robert Echlin rented the houses and a major refurbishment of the building, at the Bolton's expense, was agreed. The next document in the file is dated March 1745 and it is an estimate, submitted by a carpenter Mich Dunn for the 'necessary work' which totaled £67 19s. The works outlined were for a major refurbishment and refit of a sizeable residence. For example, the painting estimate was for 1540 square yards of painting on the outside and inside. The documents refer to a front hall, back hall, several parlours and several rooms in a servants quarter. The estimate of costs was itemised by trade, bricklayer, carpenter, glazier, slater, plumber, painter etc. The refit work was carried out during 1746 and 1747 and in March 1747 a file of the invoices from the various tradesmen was submitted to Mrs Bolton (Archbishop Bolton died in January 1744). The final statement, which totaled £111 11s. 8d., spread over ten numbered and separate categories, proposed to Mrs Bolton that it would be in order to pay the project manager Mr Edward Mathews so that he in turn could make the payments to the tradesmen. In eight cases (reference numbers three to ten) the individual invoices have survived and a detailed statement is provided of the work done, the materials used and the prices per foot or square foot/yard, pound or per day as applicable. Examples of specific prices included bricklayers who were paid 2s. a day (this implies the potential for the sizeable annual income of up to £25–£30), bricks priced at fifteen shillings per thousand and window painting costs of between 1d. and 2d. per foot of glazing bar. Some of the quantities/dimensions itemised in the file were certified as correct, in September 1746, by a Laurence Purfield. There is a receipt at the end of each invoice most of which were dated June 1747. Each was signed by the relevant tradesman, including one by the slater

4 Final statement of costs for the refurbishment of Sir Richard Echlin's house Queen Street – 1747. The final statement dated March 1747 totaled £111 11s. 8d. compared to the original March 1745 estimate of £67 19s.

Thomas Holland who was illiterate and therefore made 'his mark' on the receipt. Each receipt noted the receipt of full payment (including references to partial payment already made where applicable) from Mr Mathews.

The cost of the refurbishment of the house in Queen Street would sit well with McKellar's estimates for housing costs in London at the same time. The overall impression from the file is of a well-organised system where the tradesmen were aware of and familiar with their role in the total system and with the level of detailed information that they were expected to provide in order secure the contract in the first place and in due course to secure payment. An interesting feature of the file is the several references to the recycling of materials these included floorboards within the house and lead, which was to be sold externally, with a offsetting reduction in the bill. The archbishop of Cashel's house was returned several times in the parish paving returns in the 1730s and Sir Robert Echlin's house was returned in the paving returns of March 1745. The assumption must be that the paving to the front of the house was repaired as part of the refurbishment project as neither Sir Robert Echlin nor the Mrs Bolton were listed in the returns for 1746 and 1747.[45]

Hendrick and his fellow developers in Dublin in the early decades of the 18th century were developing these new suburbs in response to demand for quality suburban housing. Sources of this demand included the practice of country gentlemen to visit Dublin for the biennial sessions of parliament, the vice-regal season or simply to spend the winter in the city in order to avail of cultural or other facilities, such as the superior childbirth care, available in Dublin. Almost all of these visitors rented houses for the occasion, usually on a short lease, and few, except the very rich, built their own Dublin town houses. Renting in Dublin was expensive and many contemporaries noted that prices were on a par with those prevailing in London.[46] The Cosby family of Stradbally in Queen's County provides a case study of the behaviour of a well connected landed country family in this regard. Cosby noted in 1725 that his father 'took the house next to the graveyard in Stephen's Green for the six months of winter from Mrs Humming Widdow of Dr Humming and gave £50 for the house ready furnished'. In 1730 Cosby's first child was born at a house in King Street 'almost over against St Paul's'. The child was baptized in St Paul's in July of that year. In 1739 the St Paul's area was still sufficiently prestigious for Cosby when he noted that 'my wife I and family went up to Dublin to winter there, we took a whole house on Arran Quay and paid £55 for it for 6 months', unfortunately the rentier was not mentioned.[47]

How did William Hendrick finance the acquisition of and the development of such an extensive property portfolio? His inheritance of £300 from his grandfather in 1712 would have been insufficient to finance the scale of his later property development activities.[48] He secured at least some of the required resources by taking out mortgages on his various land holdings. The first mortgage transaction of William Hendrick that I have discovered to date was in 1719 when Hendrick mortgaged his Arran Quay site to a William Leeson for £300 pounds.[49] A further mortgage transaction took place in November 1723 when Hendrick borrowed £1,000 from the Rev William Williamson, the rector of the parish of St Paul since 1722.[50] While the rate of interest was not stated in every mortgage memorial a fixed annual rate of around 6 per cent seems to have been the norm with half yearly interest payments and a lump sum repayment at the end of the term, at which point the mortgage was either redeemed or renewed. A number of acts regulating the rate of interest to 6 or 7 per cent were passed by the Irish parliament in this period.[51] In March 1724 William Hendrick undertook the first of a series of mortgage transactions with Mrs Jane Bury. In this transaction Hendrick mortgaged his holding of a 'parcell of ground and strand between the wooden bridge commonly called the Bloody Bridge and the stone bridge opposite Queen Street and commonly called Ellis's Bridge situate in the parish of St Paul's Oxmantowne of the county of the city of Dublin' to Jane Bury and jointly to 'Honable Jane Moore Daughter of the right honourable John Lord Baron of Tullymoore.' Jane Bury was the widow of John Bury of Shannongrove in Limerick and daughter of William Palliser, archbishop of Cashel.[52] This mortgage was for £1,500 and no rate of interest was stated. This debt was discharged three years later and a note was inscribed in the margin of the Registry of Deeds memorial stating 'The mortgage mentioned in this memorial is satisfied and discharged as appears by a certificate under the hand and seal of the mortgagee bearing the date 9th Day of May 1727 Which certificate no. 920.'[53] In November 1726 Hendrick took out a mortgage with the same investors for the same ground and also for other parts of his land holdings in the Smithfield area including the Bowling Green and property on Tighe Street.[54] This memorial also has a later entry to the effect that the debt had been discharged under a certificate also dated 9 May 1727 and described as certificate number 921.[55] On the same day William Hendrick borrowed or re-borrowed £4,500 from the same parties using the same security with the mortgage being registered on the next day, 10 May.[56] The records in the Registry of Deeds record no release certificate for this mortgage. It appears, from later memorials, that this mortgage was replaced by a later one dated 20 August 1729, but this later mortgage does not appear to have been listed in the Registry of Deeds.[57] The Bury's were not Hendrick's only source of mortgage finance and in September 1729 William and Thomas Hendrick mortgaged property on Blind Quay to James Swift for £600.[58] These financial memorials are the partial record of a complex series of inter-related transactions involving a large number of individuals and which included Primate Boulter in Armagh as one of the providers of the source capital.

   William Hendrick encountered financial problems in the late 1720s and the early 1730s. The terms of the mortgage for £4,500 with Jane Bury were not met, and in 1729 he was taken to court by the Bury family who finally won their case in 1739. By this time the debt, including accrued interest, had increased to £6,868 11s. 8d. – this increase in the total sum due has an implied compound rate of about 5 per cent per annum for the ten years from 1729 to 1739. The result of the case was that the mortgage rights for the relevant properties were sold, at auction, to a Humphrey Minchin in 1740 for £6,800.[59] There were no recorded disposals in the memorials of the Registry of Deeds of sites in this area by Humphrey Minchin in the period 1740 to 1745. This transaction seems to have been the last involving William Hendrick in the Smithfield area of the city. However, despite this setback Hendrick did not totally disappear from the Dublin property scene. In the mid-1730s along with various members of his family, he was recorded as carrying out a series of transactions, on a substantial property inherited from John Hendrick in 1712, with Jane Bury in the Frances Street and Hanover Lane area on the south side of the city. Some of these transactions involved nominal consideration such as 'for one grain of wheat (if demanded) to the intent and purpose that the said Jane Bury may be in actual possession of the premises and to be able to accept a grant thereof'.[60]

The evolution of the urban morphology of the Smithfield area from the initial allocation of plots in the 1660s until the completion of the area nearly a century later is a story of continuous growth. This growth was managed by Dublin corporation and also by private developers, their builders, their clients and financiers. The initial plan seems to have been to develop a new high-status suburb and to that end some key components of infrastructure, as understood at that time, were developed. Key early actions in support of that vision included the granting of development lots in 1665, the land grant to the duke of Ormond, the laying out of the Bowling Green, the development of the Blue Coat School, the enquaying of the north bank of the river and the construction of or the reconstruction of two bridges. This was followed some decades later by the construction of the parish church and graveyard and the improvement of services for the provision of lighting, paving, water and local security. However, despite its initial good start, and the best efforts of William Hendrick and other property developers, the Smithfield St Paul's area did not maintain its early high-status position. The ultimate failure can be traced to a number of factors including the desire of the increasingly economically powerful middle-class to migrate to cleaner and more aesthetically pleasing single-use areas and the subsequent development of new suburbs of the city that were more in line with this evolving land use pattern. As late as 1710 the *Dublin Gazette* could report the sale of 'two large mault-houses, each of 3 floors, with good killns, steeps, water and all conveniencies, situated over-against Dr. Thomas Molyneus's dwelling house at the end of New-Row'.[61] It is unlikely that leading figures of the middle class would have continued to live in such a multi-use environment in such a confined geographical space long after this date. Land use patterns in the Smithfield area that did not sit well with this new aesthetic included the Royal Barracks and also the presence of industrial, markets and numerous taverns.[62] Other land use patterns in the area that could be considered inimical to the maintenance of a high-status area included Thwaite's malting house and the Carpenters Widdow House on the north-side of the green and the siting of the city stables and the city pipe yard in Barrack Street. The lack of a major aristocratic residence was also a negative factor. Open-air preaching was one of the purposes for which Oxmantown Green was used in the mid-eighteenth century. In 1746 and 1747 Thomas Williams and Charles Wesley from the nascent Methodist movement preached on the green, reputedly to crowds of thousands which consisted of soldiers and Dubliners of all faiths.[63]

There were two further Swiftain connections with the Smithfield St Paul's area. Stella (Esther Johnson) and her longtime companion Rebecca Dingley, or the 'Ladyes' as Swift referred to them, lived in Archdeacon Wall's house in Queen Street for extensive periods in the years 1714–17. The address on Swift's letters to Walls was usually described as 'at his House over against the Blue-coat Hospitall in Queen-Street Dublin'.[64] Twenty years later in the mid-1730s Swift contemplated locating his proposed 'hospital for lunatics and idiots' on Oxmantown Green and in 1735 he successfully petitioned Dublin corporation to grant him a site for that purpose.[65] The idea was that, in return for the granting of his legacy the city would provide a site, and also manage the hospital once constructed. The new facility was to be located close to the Blue Coat School, also under the aegis of Dublin corporation, in order to share administrative resources. However, when the corporation relaxed some of the restrictions against Presbyterians, or 'fanatics' as Swift called them, he changed his will and he set about organising an independent group of trustees to manage the new institution. Like Ormond before him Swift never built in Oxmantown and his hospital was built on a site across the river near Stevens' hospital after his death in 1745.[66]

William Hendrick was the most active property developer in the Smithfield St Paul's area in the 1720s. His many leasing agreements illustrate the complex and sophisticated conditions that were apparently standard business practice in the Dublin property, financial and rental markets at this time. They also demonstrate the deep family and business interconnections in the Dublin civic and business community of this period. Ultimately the property development business of William Hendrick failed and he was forced out of active involvement in the civic and parochial affairs of the Smithfield St Paul's neighbourhood. This did not stop the development of the area in later decades as witnessed by the encroachment of building development onto the remaining open spaces in the area throughout the remainder of the century. William Hendrick's legacy remains however in the general street layout and in some of the street names of much of the area between Smithfield and the river.

2. The vestry of St Paul's parish, 1698–1750

The parish vestry of the Church of Ireland was a significant agent of local government in 18th-century Ireland. While the burdens placed on the parish vestry in Ireland never reached the levels of responsibility allocated to parish vestries in England and Wales the civic role of the parish nevertheless grew in complexity and intrusiveness in the first half of the 18th century until it covered a wide range of matters ranging from gathering local taxes, administration of poor relief, monitoring paving and lighting services and the provision of local security. Decisions of the vestry were noted as resolutions or acts of the vestry and were recorded in the vestry minute book. They were implemented through the actions of the parish officers who were selected by the parish vestry each year at Easter-time. The rules of vestry required the presence of the minister or curate to pass these acts, which also needed a majority of those present to approve an act. Attendance at the vestry by the male cess-payers of the parish was not obligatory but the law required that every vestry act or order be entered into a parish book and signed by 'such other inhabitants present as shall think proper to sign the same'.[1]

The questions arising from an analysis of the civic role, activities, membership of and impact of the parish vestry on day-to-day life of the citizens of 18th-century Dublin is a little studied area in Irish history. Likewise the nature of the interaction between the parish vestry and other agents of local administration, Dublin Corporation in the case of the parishes in the city of Dublin, is under-explored.[2] This chapter analyses some of these issues, in the period from 1697 to c.1750 and it will do so by focussing on the activities of the parish vestry in the newly formed parish of St Paul in the rapidly expanding north-side extramural suburbs of Dublin. The actions of the parish vestry of St Paul were recorded in the first vestry minute book for the parish which covers the period from 1698 to 1750 and which is preserved in RCB Library.[3]

Until the end of the 17th century St Michan's was the only parish on the north-side of Dublin city. However, in 1697, the continuous growth in the population to the north of the river provided the impetus for the division of St Michan's and the creation of three new parishes (new St Michan's, St Paul's and St Mary's). The division of St Michan's was given effect in an act of the Irish parliament in 1697 entitled An act for divideing the Parish of St Michan's, within the City and Suburbs of Dublin, into three distinct Parishes. The act stated that 'by the late increase of buildings and inhabitants there is a cure too great to be discharged by one single minister and the parochial church is not large enough ... St Michan's shall ... be divided into several parishes'. The 1697 act defined the footprint of the new parish, named the first rector and the first churchwardens and also provided for the raising of local taxes and the allocation of a site for the construction of a new parish church and graveyard. The section in the act that outlined the footprint of the new parish is set out below:

> All those the houses and lands on the west side of Smithfield, and also an alley there, called Peter's alley, on both sides, and cross Channell-row the breath of the said Peter's alley to countess dowager of Drogheda's house, excluding the said house, and from the said countesse of Drogheda's house westward, and northward as far as the antient bounds of the parish of St. Michans do extend, and from the said west side of Smithfield southwards by the glass-house, including the said Glass-house, as also the back stables and Arrans key to Mr Thompson's house exclusively as far as the river Liffey, and thence also westward as far as the bounds of the old parish reach.[4]

The first fruits taxation for the three new parishes totaled £12 11.s. The act stated that this was to be divided between the three parishes in the ratio of St Paul's £3 (26 per cent), St Mary's £4 (35 per cent) and St Michan's £5. 11s. (48 per cent). These ratios represented the contemporary assessment of the relative wealth and income generating capacity of each of the three new parishes. It appears therefore that the area covered by the parish of St Paul was considered to be the least developed part of the north-side of the city at this time. Work commenced quickly on building the new church. The cost of the construction of St Paul's was not mentioned in the enabling act of parliament or in the vestry minute book and the *Calendar of the ancient records of Dublin* did not record a grant being given by Dublin Corporation. The new church was consecrated on Wednesday 4 April 1702 and, at the opening ceremony, a deed of gift in perpetuity for 'a seat in the Church for the Lord Mayor and his successors and a place for the Blew Boys of King Charles's Hospital' was presented as per a vestry minute of Easter Monday 1701.[5] The first meeting of the parish vestry to be held in the new church was on Tuesday 17 April 1702, prior to that date the meetings had taken place in the Blue Coat School.[6] By the end of 1702 the vestry was ready to finalise the construction phase when it noted on 10 December of 1702 that 'Thomas Ash and Ephraim Thwaites should inspect the accounts of Capt. Corker and examine what money was laid out on building the Parish Church & Church Yard etc and return wt money remains due for the work and upon what account, and wt money has not been disposed of or allowed by the act of parliament.'[7]

The new building was not apparently of any enduring architectural merit. The original building at St Paul's only lasted for 120 years before being replaced by the present structure.[8] The regular references in the vestry minutes to roof repairs, from the early years of the 18th century, may indicate that there was some flaw in the original workmanship or perhaps even in the original design. To date no visual images of the original St Paul's church have been found.[9] In his, *Historical guide to ancient and modern Dublin*, published in 1821, Wright described the original St Paul's as a 'rude specimen of architecture' with 'three rugged stone walls, few windows and they disproportionate to the size of the building' and an 'enormous roof of an extravagant pitch'. This may have accounted for the constant roofing bills. The interior was described as being spacious with a three-sided gallery and an organ at the west-end, but overall in a 'ruinous and miserable condition.'[10]

The granting of permission to the leading citizens in the parish for the construction of family burial vaults began as early November 1700, before the church was finished, when it was agreed that Edward Corker (one of the first set of churchwardens referred to in the enabling act) 'shall have liberty to make a vault twenty foot square on the East side of the Church Yard ... Paying five shillings a year'. In April 1705 Henry Westenra was allowed to build a vault and in October of that year Thomas Tilson was allowed to build a vault.[11] In 1719 the parish decided to add a chancel and vestry room to the church and the parish approached the city assembly for support.[12] The city assembly gave its permission for this and also for some associated works in the following terms:

> Pursuant to the above order we, the committee, have examined the within petition, and are of opinion that the petitioners have for the use of the within (named) parish nine foot in breath into the north wall, and sixteen foot in length at the east end of the church, to build a vestry room on, and that they have liberty of a sweep for coaches to turn in, provided they build walls on the east and west ends of the church from the church-yard wall to the street wall, and making turnstiles with sufficient grates, to be kept in order and repair by the parish: and that the said parish, in consideration of the said ground and liberty aforesaid, be obliged to continue the seats which the boys of the Blew coat Hospital use to them for the future: which we submit to your honours, this 2nd June, 1719.[13]

The record of the activities of and the composition of the vestry of St Paul's parish provides a case study of the functioning of, and the personalities involved in, parish vestries in Dublin in the early decades of the eighteenth century. These records also provide a means for assessing the impact of the local parish vestry on the local community and also for assessing the involvement of the local elite in the detailed civic and ecclesiastical work of the parish vestry. The inhabitants of the parish of St Paul included some titled citizens; for example, Lord Charlemont was a church warden in 1701 and there were also a number of parishioners who were prominent in the business, governmental and political scene in this period.[14] The latter included Thomas Keightley, Richard Tighe, Thomas Tilson and Alan Brodrick.[15] However, as already noted the social status of the parish of St Paul's declined until, by the end of the 18th century, its status, as measured by the proportion of upperclass inhabitants, addresses of peers and members of parliament, owners of sedan chairs and the location of up-market retailers such as perfumers, gold and silversmiths and print and booksellers was surpassed by the north-side suburbs of Sackville Street, Henrietta Street and Rutland Square and by St Stephen's Green on the south side.[16] Most of the men who participated in the vestry of St Paul's or who filled the various parish offices (with the exception of a joint sextonship held by Sarah Sharples only men feature as activists within the parish records of St Paul's at this time) were therefore not well-known or figures of national significance.[17]

Notwithstanding the survival of many 18th-century vestry minute books our understanding of the working of this important local institution is still incomplete.[18] From the middle of the 17th century the practice grew up in London for smaller meetings of parishioners to be called to consider decisions that did not involve the entire parish. This smaller group became known as the select vestry and it is not clear if the Dublin parishes adopted this practice in this period.[19] When historians have analysed the minutes of vestry meetings in Dublin in this period the presence of relatively small numbers of signatures in minute books has presented a problem of interpretation.[20] Was this a sign of the operation of a select vestry or was it an indicator of apathy and a low level of civic participation by the local elite in the management of parish affairs? For example, in the case of St Paul's parish there was an average of only 10.7 signatures appended to the minutes of the 33 meetings of the parish vestry in the first ten years of its existence. One possible interpretation of this data is that the small numbers of signatures appended to minutes could be the result of a practice of using only samples of those present to certify the formal record of decisions arrived at during the meeting. For example there is a record of such an occurrence in 1683 in the parish of St Bride where a memorandum of a meeting to discuss church repairs, which had fourteen signatures appended to it, noted that the meeting was attended by 'near three score of the chief inhabitants'. The discrepancy was explained as being due to the fact that the majority could not wait for the decisions to be 'fairly transcribed'.[21] However, the explicit recording of this fact could be interpreted as showing the unusual nature of only using a sample of those present and therefore to imply that a complete list of signatures for those present was the normal practice. The St Bride's minute also implies that it was practice to write out the minute at the end of the meeting and for the book then to be signed by those in attendance, or at least the majority that agreed with the motions carried. The layout of the St Paul's minute book implies that there was a similar practice in that parish.

The St Paul's vestry minute book contains evidence from 1731 to indicate that the number of signatures appended to a minute was in fact an accurate reflection of the actual attendance at the meeting in question. In the course of a dispute with the lord mayor over the appointment of a parishioner, Martin Norton, as a constable, a vestry presentment to the King's Bench noted 'That we the Minister, Churchwardens and Parishioners of the said parish being assembled in a vestry in the said parish to the number of Fifteen: Did on Easter Tuesday last being the twentieth day of April 1731'.[22] The fifteen attendees mentioned in this entry tallies with the number of signatures appended to the minute of the 20 April 1731 meeting as inscribed in the minute book. This would seem to indicate that the attendance at vestry meetings was small and consisted only of the individuals whose signatures were appended at the bottom of the relevant minute. The appearance of the same names at the foot of the minutes of meeting after meeting, often stretching over many years, would also argue against the view that there was a practice of only using sample signatures or of minutes being signed only by those who agreed with the motion. Given the importance of the matters being decided, in particular the raising of parish cess and the appointment of parish officers who had extensive local powers, it would not be unreasonable to expect a higher number of attendees at the Easter meeting (effectively a form of AGM). However, in the case of St Paul's parish the number of signatures on minutes for the Easter vestry in the first ten years, at an average of 11.3 per Easter meeting, was only marginally higher that the overall average for the period as a whole. Finally there is no direct evidence in the minutes of the parish of St Paul in the period 1698–1750, such as the use of the term select, or any similar term, of the appointment of a select vestry from within the general body of parishioners.

Because of the civic nature of many of the responsibilities of the parish the issue of the right to attend and vote at parish vestry meetings affected not just the conformists of the established church but it also had an impact on the wider local community including non-conformist protestants and Roman Catholics. In theory, the heads of all households (including Roman Catholics and non-conformists) could attend, participate, vote and be office-holders of the vestry. The potential for Roman Catholics and dissenters to attend and vote at meetings in defence of their interest – for example by voting against the raising of taxes to support the maintenance of the fabric of churches of the Church of Ireland – resulted, in the mid-1720s, in Roman Catholics being statutorily debarred from voting in vestries convened to sanction church repairs.[23] The eligibility for the post of churchwarden was ill-defined although some parishioners, such as clergy, peers, lawyers and members of parliament were excluded by virtue of their position. In theory all other cess-payers in the parish were eligible to serve. Despite this exemption Richard Tighe (who was an MP) served as churchwarden in St Paul's for three years in the mid-1720s.[24] Many of the parish roles were rotated among the parish activists so that, over time, a high proportion of the male population of the area would have served the parish, and hence their local community, in some function. For example, 117 individuals were nominated for the roles of director of the watch, constable or watchman in St Paul's in the ten years after 1721.[25] The position of churchwarden was a significant local office and in 1730 a book describing the duties of churchwardens by Dr Humphrey Prideaux, the leading English Anglican controversialist, was advertised on a number of occasions in the *Dublin Gazette*: 'Lately printed and sold by the printer hereof, Dr Prideaux's Direction to Churchwardens for the Faithful Discharge of their Office. N.B. This book was printed by the direction of his grace the late Arch-Bishop of Dublin and recommended by him at visitations.'[26] The use of this book in Dublin would seem to imply that the roles and responsibilities of churchwardens in England and Ireland were sufficiently similar to allow the use of an English text as guidance for churchwardens in Dublin.

Barnard is of the view that participation in the parish vestry and acting as parish officers may have helped the middling sort to distinguish themselves from the lower ranks. This involvement, both by the middling sort and by the members of the more powerful local families, could be motivated by a number of factors such as religious zeal or more worldly concerns to do with the exercise of local power or the preservation of local status or privilege.[27] As in many local communities it is possible to see a local dynamic at work where of a coterie of activists and involved individuals were at the heart of most activities in the area. The records of the surviving Dublin vestry minute books – and those for the parish of St Paul are no exception to this pattern – show that the same names regularly signed the minute book, undertook the various parish offices, and occupied some of the best pews in church. They therefore formed an exclusive group, or coalition of the willing. Many were already prominent in their neighbourhood and who could use their tenure of parochial office to consolidate their existing authority. There is also however, evidence of numbers of illiterate parishioners participating, at least in minor roles, in the parish structures.[28] Given that the conforming community nationally consisted of only a small minority of the entire population this activism in the parish became an additional mark distinguishing the activist conformist from their uninvolved Roman Catholic, dissenter and non-participating conformist neighbours.

The vestry minutes of many parishes, and especially the early minutes, contain little detail. Meetings were relatively infrequent, for example there was only an average of 3.3 vestry meetings per annum in the first ten years in St Paul's parish.[29] It may be the case that the minutes of parish vestries only record more important items such as those decisions that were required to be recorded by church canons, or by statute, or where there was a clear need to keep formal written records for possible use, or even inspection, at a future date. The first meeting of the vestry of St Paul's parish was held, 'before the church was built', in the Blue Coat School on 26 April 1698. The text of this first entry is set out below:

> Saint Pauls Parish
> At a meeting of the said parish, before the church was built, Upon the 26th day of April 1698. William Wells who was chosen by Mr Burridge the minister & licens'd by the Archbishop of Dublin to be Clarke during his good Behaviour, was approv'd of by the Parishioners. And it was then agreed & hereby declar'd that William Sharp shall be Sexton to the said Parish during his good behaviour. It is also further resolvd that Edward Edwards shall be Bedle of the said Parish. And whereas the Common beggars frequenting this City a perfect nuisance, it is agreed that a true & certain list be made of all the poor now inhabiting this parish, and [ms illegible] such as are really so shall be admitted.[30]

Uniquely in the first minute book of St Paul's parish, no signatures were attached to this entry. The appointment of parish officers was the main purpose of the meeting and this task remained a preoccupation of vestry meetings throughout the period. At the next meeting of the vestry, held a year later on 10 April 1699, Edwards was replaced as beadle by John Adams who was to 'be allowed a Gown, a Capp and a Staff and twelve pence a week'. A year later in 1700 it was noted that 'John Adams Beadle of this psh be allowed a salary of three pounds Sterl p annum and that from this day he be admitted as one of the poore of this psh'. In this instance the vestry may have been using its modest patronage as a means of relieving distress as well as having a key parish function carried out. It is also apparent from the signatures of the meeting of March 1703 that Adams was illiterate as his entry in the book for that meeting was 'The Mark of X John Adams Beadle'.[31] Adams continued in the role of Beadle for many years and the job may have become something of an Adams family sinecure. In September 1716 it was recorded that John Adams was to replace his father, of the same name, as Beadle and, over twenty years later, at a meeting on 25 May 1738, it was minuted that 'Andrew Adams be beadle of this parish in the room of his brother William Adams deceased and that he have the same employees sallary as his brother enjoyed'.[32] The job of sexton also appears to have been a family affair. On 24 June 1709 a minute noted 'that Sarah Sharples and

John Sharples her son do jointly succeed in the place of Sexton to the Parish of St Paul's in the Room of William Sharples Dec.d or the survivor.'[33]

The sale of pews, or seats as they were almost always referred to in the minute book, was a recurring topic at vestry meetings in St Paul's parish. While the seating capacity of St Paul's church is not known, given the number of pews (53), it cannot have been more than three to four hundred (i.e. 53 pews by approximately six or seven occupants per pew) and this figure is very similar to an estimate for St Paul's listed in Monk Mason's manuscript in the Dublin City Archives.[34] Possession of a seat in church came only after making a payment and the seating lists as transcribed into the vestry minute book of St Paul's parish show that the seat-paying public in the new parish were dominated by the parish activists. In March 1701, approximately one year before the church was opened it was agreed that 'the seats in the Gallery of the Church of the Sd. Parish shall be disposed of to the severall parishioners and at the Rates above mentioned and that the money be paid in immediately to the Church Wardens towards finishing the seats and the church'.[35] This minute listed 21 gallery pew holders, who between them contributed a total of £173 10s. 0d. The prices paid for seats varied from a modest £2 up to £15 paid by lords Charlemont and Drogheda. Leading parish activists of the time who paid for pews at this early date included Philip Craven (two pews one at £2 10s. and one at £5), Bruen Worthington £8 and Henry Westenra £11. Prices reflected the placing of the pew, with the best position being reserved for those who paid the most. In 1703 a second list of 33 seats described as 'ground seats' was transcribed into the book. Parishioners on this second list included regular vestry minute signatories such as John Green £7, James Brownlow £9 and Owen Rion £6. The total income received by the parish for the sale of these ground seats was £131 12s. This was an average of nearly £4 4s., per seat compared to a price of just over £8 5s. average for the gallery seats.

The details of seat transfers and payments for seats was recorded on a regular basis in the minutes. As the seats were transferable by the owner, they became in effect a personal asset, and the minutes record several instances where sums were paid by the new seat-holders to the family of a deceased parishioner. Eventually the vestry wished to reclaim the right to allocate the pews as it saw fit and also to retain the income. For example in March 1708 John Peyton secured seat number 15 on the ground floor, having paid £6 to the daughter of Daniel Huston deceased. However, the seat was allocated to Peyton only until his death or that of his wife, whichever was the later, and the right to the seat was then to be disposed of by the parish.[36] In 1716 a dispute arose on the question of whether the vestry had the power to sell seats in the parish church to people living outside of the parish. The parish sought a legal opinion and in the front of the minute book, on a separate sheet of paper but bound into the volume, a handwritten legal opinion from a Justice Gore dealt with this issue. Justice Gore was listed in the May 1731 paving return as living in King Street opposite the Green.[37] In March 1703 Alderman Stephens had paid £11 for a seat in the gallery. However, even at this early date there was an indication that Stevens, and the vestry, were aware of potential problems and a special meeting of the vestry was held in April 1703, attended by only seven parishioners, at which a single resolution was passed stating that 'Alderman Stevens of Stoney Batter shall hold his seat for which he paid his money and which be valued on the same condition on which the rest of the parishioners hold their respective seats'. Gore's legal opinion on the matter was that because Stevens (and his executor/s) was not a resident of the parish he was not entitled to a seat in church. Gore also concluded however that Stevens was entitled to be repaid the money that he had already paid for the seat. Alderman Stevens died sometime before July 1710 and his house 'in Stony-Batter, with the Coach-house, Garden, and Stables, and that part of the House wherein Mr Abraham White lately dwelt, with the Garden, Coach-house and Stable (are to be Let:)' was advertised in the *Dublin Gazette* in the Summer of that year.[38] The property does not however appear to have found a ready market and some months later in March 1711 it was re-advertised at 'a cheaper rate than formerly proposed.'[39] While some parts of Stoneybatter were within the parish boundary of St Paul's, Alderman Stevens residence may not have been. Stevens was not recorded as a vestry signatory at any time in the first ten years of minutes of vestry meetings. In 1716 a new list of the seats described 'as they are numbered and valued' for both the gallery and for the ground floor was prepared and transcribed into the minute book.[40] The ground floor list had 31 seats with a total value of £184 4s. 8d. while 22 seats were listed for the gallery with a value of £215, giving an overall total of 53 seats with a total value of £399 4s. 8d. Seats on the ground floor had an average value of £6 2s. 10d.(per priced seat) while those on the gallery had an average value of £9 15s. 5d. Most of the seats were occupied either by titled parishioners or by the parish activists. Seat-holders of note on the gallery included Richard Tighe (£10), Henry Westenra (£19), Bruen Worthington (£8) and Mr William Hendrick (£9).[41] A number of seats on both the ground floor and the gallery were divided between two holders.

 The organisation of the parish watch became a statutory obligation of parish vestries in Dublin following the enactment of new legislation in 1721. The watch system that was put in place in the 1720s lasted for over sixty years until its replacement in 1786.[42] Under the new law the parishes were obliged, in February of each year, to elect directors of the watch and the watchmen and to make bye-laws concerning the duties, wages and weapons of the watch. They were also obliged to present the names of the constables selected to serve in the coming year for the approval of and swearing in by the lord mayor. Richard Tighe, a St Paul's parishioner, regular attendee at vestry meetings and MP, moved the motion in the Irish parliament for the 1721 bill. He then served on the watch committee in the parish from its inception until the mid-1740s.[43] The considerable energy spent on managing the parish watch system at a local level is evidence of a concern on the part of the property-owning elite of the Smithfield area about the incidence of, or at least the perceived incidence of, crime. Unfortunately the St Paul's vestry minutes make no reference to the nature of, or the incidence of, crime that occurred within the parish. Contemporary newspapers convey only limited information on the specific nature of crime during this period. While there were frequent references in the newspapers to lost and stolen items (including pets, horses and bank drafts and bank bills) and also to deserters from the army, some of whom were shot on Oxmantown Green, there were few references to crime against the person or crimes against property.[44] In May 1728 the *Dublin Intelligence* noted that 'On Thursday night, some villains broke into the Nunnery in Channel-Row, and carry'd off several valuable goods belonging to the young ladies who board there'. The *Dublin Gazette* in July 1739 also reported that 'Last week upon a false information of arms being lodg'd in the Boarding Schools of Channel-row and King's street the same was searched but none could be found.'[45]

The parish of St Paul seems to have been assiduous in fulfilling its obligations under the parish watch legislation and from 1722 onwards the vestry minutes regularly recorded the selection of the directors of the watch committee and the nominations for constables and watchmen. The first directors were appointed in February 1722 when it was noted that:

> At a vestry then held pursuant to an act of parliament for Regulating of the watch over the inhabatance of the parish of St Paul's Did Chuse the following persons to be Comisioners for regulating the watch of the said parish Mr Thomas Tailor Bart. Richard Warbutton Esq. Richard Tighe Esq. Coll. Breach, Thomas Tilson Esq., Mr Phillip Creavan, Mr Bruen Worthington, Mr John Curtis, Mr James Brownlow, Mr Francis Anderson, Mr Wmn. Hendrick, Mr John Connor, Mr John Davis, Hen. Burrows. Mr Anthony Godfrey.[46]

This group comprised many of the leading activists in the parish in this period and it also included such leading figures as Thomas Taylor (earl of Bective) and Bruen Worthington neither of whom served on later boards of directors and neither of whom were involved in other parish activities at this time. In almost every year from 1722 onwards the minute book recorded the parish as having held meetings to approve the watch bye-laws and to confirm that the appropriate numbers of watch houses, constables, watchmen, stands and the patrolling routines were in place. For example, in March 1722 (in a typical entry) the minutes noted the watch bye-laws as:

their Stands be as follows One Man at the North End of Smithfield, one at the South End and one by Mr Thwaites's by Stoney Batter. And that the Grand Watch House be that adjoining to Ellis Bridge. That Four pounds be allowed for Watch Coats, Two pounds for Arms and four pounds for Coals, Candles & Lanthorns and fore pounds a piece be allowed for each Watch Man's Sallary for one whole year. And that Five Constables are a sufficient number for the said Parish.[47]

The expenditure on the watch that year totaled £26 which would equate to about one third of the annual parish expenditure as recorded in the churchwardens accounts in the 1730s. William Hendrick and Richard Tighe served as directors of the watch throughout the 1720s (Tighe continued to serve until the early 1740s) and William Hendrick's support for the work of the parish watch extended to the point where he financed the construction of one of the two watch houses in the parish. The entry for the vestry meeting of Wednesday 20 October 1724 noted:

> the watch house for the said parish near Ellis bridge be removed to such place as the Directors of the watch or the majority of them shall approve of to be erected at the expense of Mr William Hendrick & until such house be erected that the said Mr William Hendrick shall allow the kitchen under the Bowling Green house for a watch house.[48]

The two watch houses located in St Paul's parish were shown on the Rocque map of 1756.[49] Maintenance of the fabric of the watch house became another parish responsibility and in the accounts of 1732 it was noted 'To Mr Tho. Mease for pointing the Church and Watch House 13s. 10d.'[50]

Under an act of 1723 the occupants of the position of constables had to be approved by and sworn in by the lord mayor. In the mid-1720s St Paul's parish seems had difficulty in finding candidates who could secure the requisite approval. An entry of 23 May 1723 noted that 'Robert Bouchier was elected constable in the room of Mr Ep Thwaites who was disapproved of by the Lord Mayor without any reason given.' On Easter Tuesday 30 March 1725 the constables nominated by the parish vestry were John Moor, Richard Fitzsymmons, Cornelius Martin, David Jones and Charles Miller. However, three further special meetings, in the space of only four weeks, were required to secure final approval from the lord mayor. The sequence of events was that at a meeting on 5 July 1725 'Richard Mc Caughry was chosen constable for the present year in the room of David Jones who was disapprove'd of by the Ld. Mayor'. A week later on 12 July 1725 it was noted that 'Laurence Maguire was chosen Constable for the present year in the room of Ri Fitzimons who was disapproved of' and finally on 2 Aug 1725 it was noted that 'Daniel Maher constable in the room of L Maguire who was

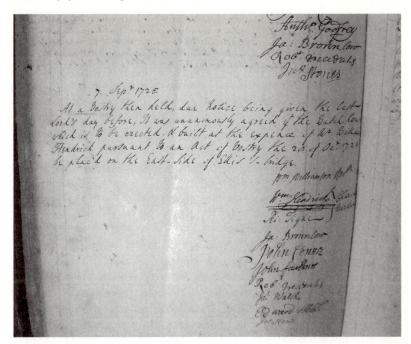

5 St Paul's Parish vestry minute book October 1724 – minute recording the location of the watch house paid for by William Hendrick on Ellis bridge. Courtesy of RCB.

dissapr'd of'. These meetings had six, eleven and twelve signatures respectively and the attendees included many leading parish activists such as Hendrick, Tighe, Brownlow and Burrows. At one point the vestry seems to have given up attempting to select constables who meet with the lord mayor's criteria and in 1729 they sent a list to the lord mayor 'in order to chose three constables out of 'em for the present year to wit. John Perry, James McDonnagh, Ri. Fitzsimons, Martin Norton and Mic. McGar'.[51] The system appears to have been a form of vetting process, controlled by the lord mayor, albeit not a particularly open or transparent one.

   In 1731 the parish became involved in a further dispute with the lord mayor over the appointment of a parish constable. The parish vestry wished to nominate someone who was unwilling to serve himself but who wished to nominate a deputy to serve in his place as allowed by the relevant act. However, the parish's nominee sought the exemption in a way that the vestry, or at least the directors of the watch, felt was outside the letter of the law. Much of the relevant correspondence dealing with this matter was transcribed into the minute book. The minute of 20 April 1731 noted the appointment of Martin Norton as constable hand a copy of the summons from the lord mayor to swear in the parish constables was then inscribed into the book.[52] The next day the minister and churchwardens received a note from the lord mayor refusing Norton and a copy of this was also transcribed into the minute book. Two weeks later the vestry appealed to the lord chief justice and set out their case in great detail in a long presentment the text of which was also transcribed into the minute book. The basis of the parish's case was that because Norton's application was late he had not validly excused himself from the duty to serve in strict compliance with the provisions of the act. The vestry was of the view that his long-term residency in the area and status as a householder required him to serve and the fact that Norton was both elderly and a Roman Catholic were not seen as sufficient grounds to exclude him. There were no further records on this matter in the minute book until nearly a year later when the minute for the meeting of 11 April 1732 noted that Norton was again nominated as constable. A month later in May 1732 it was reported that 'at a meeting of the Directors and Parishioners the following deputy constables were appointed in place of the constables selected on Easter Tuesday last for Martin Norton – William Adams' (William Adams was probably the parish beadle).[53] The desire of the vestry to nominate Norton is an example of the way in which the vestry sought to spread the burden of civic duty as widely as possible across the entire parish elite. Norton was apparently acceptable as a constable, or at least to have the burden of finding a deputy, imposed upon him, because of his standing in the community which derived from his relative wealth and his status as a householder. Apparently his advanced age and Roman Catholic religion did not constitute a sufficient barrier, at least to his nomination. Likewise the lord mayor's refusal in 1731 was based on Norton having secured a derogation from having to serve and not on the basis of his religion or his age. This incident constitutes a further illustration of the use of the minute book as a document of record for major issues affecting the civic role of the parish or where there was a potential for subsequent investigation, or inspection or even litigation.

The parish vestry was pressed into further civic duties when it was required to make returns of the condition of paving (and later of lighting) within the parish boundary. In 1729 a new act required the churchwardens and directors of watches to perambulate the streets of their respective parishes four times a year and to make a return on the condition of the paving to the lord mayor.[54] They were also required to enter the results in their vestry minute books. Under the act, the lord mayor was given power to fix street levels, to order residents to make good the paving outside their house on pain of being applotted for the cost of repairs. The first item bound into the minute book of St Paul's is the printed proclamation, of the city paving instructions of 1730.[55] This ordinance listed the requirements of the new act including the requirement to perambulate the streets in the first week of February, May, September and November each year and to make a return, to the lord mayor, within six days. Between 1730 and 1740 the minute book records the parish of St Paul as having made 12 such returns. The September 1730 return was headed:

> To the Rt. Hon. Ble the Lord Mayor of the City of Dublin. A return of the severall Parishioners and Proprietors of the severall Houses in the said Parish whose pavements are deficient and in bad repair in the said Parish pursuant to an act of Parliament made last September. September 7th 1730 The parish of St Paul's Dublin.[56]

The number of 'parishioners and proprietors' returned in this way varied from a high of 115 in the May 1733 return to a low of only 26 in the October 1740 return. The average number for the 12 returns examined was 60.5. The individual listings consisted of the street name, the name of the inhabitant of a building where a deficient pavement was returned and the number of yards of street frontage involved. On a small number of returns comments were inserted on individual lots or streets. The names listed were described as 'inhabitants' yet some names appear more than once in the same return.[57] One possible interpretation is that where an individual was listed for more than one address the perambulators recorded the name of the ground landlord because the lot in question was not, at the time of the perambulation, leased to an identified lessee and was therefore either unoccupied or undeveloped. From the returns it is possible to identify streets where particular individuals lived, or at least owned property, and also to draw some tentative conclusions on the state of development of particular streets at particular dates. It is also possible to cross-reference these names and dates with the evidence form the lease memorials in the Registry of Deeds. However, because of the above issues, it is not possible to compile street directories from these paving returns. The returns only highlight paving that was deemed to be deficient and it is likely that there were at least some houses where the paving was adequate. The variation in the names listed from one return to the next would seem to imply that the perambulators took pains to only list paving that failed to meet the criteria set out in the act and that where the householder had taken some remedial action to address the deficiencies since the previous return they did not appear in later returns. Given the yardage mentioned on the returns it would appear however, that, in many streets, the deficient paving accounted for a significant portion of many of the streets in the neighbourhood.

Nevertheless it is possible to infer some conclusions from these returns. Firstly, the returns are corroborative evidence of the continued presence of at least some upper-class residents in the Smithfield area in the 1730s. Their continued residency is confirmed by the listing of individuals such as Lady Gormanston, Lady Butler, Lady Middleton, Lord Palmerston, Dean Percival,

6 St Paul's Parish vestry minute book – paving return 7 May 1733. Courtesy of RCB.

bishop of Derry, the archbishop of Cashel, Madame Palliser (widow of a previous archbishop of Cashel), Alderman Gratten, Sir Robert Echlin and Lady Kingsland in one or more of the returns for the period. In addition to the gentry mentioned above leading parish activists such as William Hendrick, Richard Tighe, various members of the Westenra family and Bruen Worthington were reported to the lord mayor during the 1730's, some of them on more than one occasion. City institutions were not spared the potential embarrassment of being reported, or the potential expense of having to make good deficient paving. The May 1731 return listed 13 separate streets with the largest number of entries being listed for Queen Street, King Street and Tighe Street with 27, 15 and 13 names listed respectively.[58] Surprisingly no entries were listed for Smithfield on this return and Smithfield did not feature prominently in the lists throughout the 1730s although there was an entry for a Mr Thomas Hulett in the September 1731 return.[59] At various times in the 1730s the Blue Coat School, the City Stables and the paving opposite Oxmantown Green were included in returns. The returns also imply that the last remaining open boundary of Oxmantown Green, that along Arbour Hill, was not well maintained by the corporation. Comments on various returns included 'the green wall returned to the city as in the last', 'before the green belonging to the city', 'From Mr Callans Malt House to the Carpenters Charity House' 'my Lord Mayor annucance returned several times and never mended'.[60] In response to this situation in 1735 the parish allocated over £6 of its own resources to 'the benefit of Oxmantown Green'.[61]

Prior to 1729 the details of the expenditure incurred by the parish were not inscribed into the minute book on a regular bases (some minor detail was inscribed from time to time). From 1729 the churchwardens' accounts were included each year, however the data inscribed excluded money spent on poor relief, the watch and also perhaps on other parish outgoings. The sources of income and the details of the parish cess were not shown as these were recorded in a separate cess book that has apparently not survived.[62] The expenditure listed in these accounts was of four types viz. payments for 'King's Bench and Tholsel Presentments', salaries for parish officials (sexton, beadle, clerke, perambulators and cess collectors), expenditure on building and fabric maintenance and expenditure on supplies for church services and parish administration. The general pattern of expenditure was constant throughout the 1730s. The expenses incurred for the King's Bench and Tholsel Presentments represented the single largest category of expenditure in most years accounting for between 15 per cent and 47 per cent of total expenditure in any given year and an average of 36 per cent of expenditure in the nine years in which it was recorded.[63] The 1731 a listing of parish moveable assets records 'one book for entering Kings Bench presentments' however this book does not appear to have survived. The practice of parishes being involved in and incurring costs associated with the pleadings at the Tholsel court and at King's Bench can be traced back to at least 1691. In that year the churchwardens' accounts for the parish of St Catherine noted 'Paid for taking an indictment in (tolsel) £1 9s.' and also 'Paid for an indictment in King's Bench £2 11s.'[64] St Paul's parish incurred expense for this item from at least 1718 when the Easter vestry entry for that year noted 'The sum of forty pounds be applotted in and levied from the several inhabitants of the said parish for payment of the sum of eleven pounds eight shillings and nine pence halfpenny for several cases ordered by warrant from the Lord Mayor pursuant to several presentments at the King's Bench and Quarter Sessions.'[65] Overall the average annual parish expenditure on items other than the King's Bench presentments for the eleven years from 1729 to 1739 was just over £55 12s. This included expenditure on bread and wine for the sacrament, candles and Psalters, prayer books and account books, registers and copies of Acts of Parliament. This last expenditure reflected the need of the vestry and the parish officers to stay abreast of the increasingly onerous requirements being imposed on them in this period. In 1732 the vestry book itself features in the accounts when the parish spent, the not inconsiderable sum of eight shillings and four pence which was described as 'To Mr Jo. Wattson bill for binding this book & for a cess book'.[66]

In 1707 the parish organised a collection for the relief of distress of the inhabitants of Lisburn following a major fire in that town. The last page of the minute book lists the 104 individuals who contributed a total of £18 15s. 3d. for this cause. The size of donations varied from £1 3s. from Lord Drogheda, Lord Blessington and Thomas Keightley to more modest amounts donated by the likes of 'three servants' who donated 6d., a Thomas Mallon and a Margaret Kelly who donated 2d. each and a Catherine Carroll who donated 1d. Other contributions included 18s. 6d. from Richard Tighe, Henry Westenra and James Brownlow. Ephraim Thwaites, Thomas Tilson, Thomas Ashe and Edward Corker contributed 5s. 5d. each and the rector Charles Carr contributed 9s. 3d.[67] The similarity of the amounts donated by many of those listed would imply that a range of 'acceptable' contributions, perhaps set by social status, had been specified in advance.

The vestry minute book of the parish of St Paul in Dublin provides an insight, not only into the way in which the local activists managed the fabric and finance of their church building and facilities, but also into the workings of a major local institution for the civic government of Dublin in the early 18th century. As such the vestry minutes constitute an important ecclesiastical, civic, social and business record. In the first ten years of St Paul's parish the vestry minute book listed individual names on over 500 occasions (the number of individuals involved cannot be readily determined but it was probably over 100). The case for the publication of these records of local civic life is well illustrated by the stories that have been told in this chapter. These include evidence that the relatively small numbers of signatures inscribed in vestry minute books in this period was an accurate reflection of the actual numbers of attendees at these meetings. These records also reveal that all aspects of the process of nomination, approval and disapproval of parish constables was well understood by all concerned and that it seems to have been adhered to in a form more or less in line with legislation. There is evidence of a well-organised bureaucracy at work with numerous items of correspondence on a wide variety of issues going forwards and backwards between the different parties on a range of local issues. The expenditure accounts reveal that the parish expenditure was a relatively modest average of £76 per-annum in the 1730s spread across a wide variety of expenditure categories. This amount constituted the annual rental for between two and three houses in the neighbourhood using the rental agreement between William Hendrick and the rector, the Revd William Williamson, as a benchmark.[68]

3. The local elite of the Smithfield St Paul's area

The individuals who constituted the local elite in the Smithfield St Paul's area in the early decades of the eighteenth century knew one another intimately, they were connected by parochial, civic, business and family ties. This chapter gives brief biographies of four leading parishioners and of the first three clergymen of St Paul's parish.

Bruen Worthington Bruen Worthington was actively involved in the work of the parish at its formation in 1698 and for the first eight years thereafter. He signed the minutes for 11 vestry meetings before 1706. He was later briefly involved as a director of the watch in 1722.[1] His activities in the parish included being listed as a 'valuater of the land tax' in 1699 and as a sidesman in 1700.[2] He was recorded as having purchased a seat on the north-side of the church for £8 in March 1701 and he was still recorded as the owner of seat number 47, valued at the same amount, in 1716.[3] He was also one of the churchwardens in both 1704 and 1705. In the wider world of administration and government in Dublin Bruen Worthington was admitted to the franchise of the city in 1696 as a brewer.[4] He was Deputy Registrar of the Registry of Deeds from 1708 until 1715 in which role he signed and apparently transcribed, the handwriting appears to match that of his signature in the vestry minutes of St Paul's, the memorials from number three onwards.[5] He also acted as the notary public for memorial number two. The first two memorials in the register were signed by the registrar B. Parry. In November 1715 a William Parry replaced Worthington as the deputy registrar and he signed the entries in the ledgers from entry number 6893 onwards.[6] William Parry was a clerk to Bruen Worthington before 1715, being recorded as such in the will of William Brabazon of Co. Louth in May 1714.[7] In 1716 Bruen Worthington and Isaac Ambrose purchased the office of clerk of the House of Commons in a complicated two-stage transaction. This transaction involved Thomas Tilson the elder, a parishioner of St Paul's, who had had the role of clerk since the reign of Charles II and also Thomas Tilson the younger, selling the sinecure to Thomas Trotter and Francis Skiddy who in turn sold it to Worthington and Ambrose. The transaction had the support of the commons which noted that 'they being persons very well qualified for that imployment and very acceptable to the said house as witnessed our hands this 20 day of June 1716.'[8] In his role as clerk of the House of Commons

Worthington authorised the issuing of the printed versions of the sermons of the chaplains of the house including the sermon of Charles Carr, then rector of St Paul's, for the 30 January 1716.[9] Aspects of changes to Worthington's family can be traced through the parish register of St Paul's. On 29 September 1700 the baptism of a John Worthington was noted and on 16 March 1707 the baptism of Grace, daughter of Bruen and Mary Worthington, was noted. Bruen Worthington's funeral was recorded for 23 December 1736 and that of his wife Mary only four days earlier on 19 December 1736.[10]

Henry Westenra   Henry Westenra was a member of a prominent local property-owning family. His father Warner Westenra was one of the original grantees from the 1665 allocation of plots in Smithfield where he was granted plots numbers 96 and 97. These plots were located adjacent to the site on which the parish church of St Paul's parish was built over thirty years later. The Blue Coat school records show that in 1729 a Henry Westenra was in possession of these two plots. Henry Westenra was one of the first churchwardens named in the act that established the new parish. Previously he had been a parishioner of St Michan's and his wife was buried in that church in May 1700.[11] In the spring of 1701 he was appointed to a group that was tasked, on behalf of the parish, 'Along with wardens and sidesmen to inspect finishing of the church'.[12] Also in 1701, prior to the opening of the church, he purchased a seat on the South side of the gallery for £11.[13] He was a regular signatory at vestry meetings from 1700 onwards. In April 1705 he was allowed to sink a vault for his family in the church. Mason recorded a donation of £50 to the parish in 1719 although there was no record of his burial in St Paul's in 1718 or 1719.[14]

Richard Tighe   Richard Tighe was a contemporary of William Hendrick on the vestry of St Paul's parish in the mid-1720s when they served as churchwardens for the three years from 1723 to 1725, at a time when it was unusual for churchwardens to serve more than one year. He was director of the watch for the parish from 1722 until 1740. Richard Tighe was the grandson of Alderman Richard Tighe, lord mayor of Dublin in 1651, 1652 and 1655 and a member of the Cromwellian parliament in 1656. Richard Tighe the younger was a well-connected political and business figure and, in 1741, his grandson William was the first of the Tighe family to buy into property in Ashford Co. Wicklow. The Tighe's continued as landlords in Rossanagh in Ashford until the 1930s. The Tighe family was closely associated with the mission of John Wesley in Ireland and several members of the family were MPs for Wicklow in the eighteenth and nineteenth centuries. The Tighe connection in the area is evidenced by the local reference to the (pre-motorway) road from Rathnew to Ashford as Tighe's Avenue.[15] The elder Richard Tighe established the Bowling Green in

Oxmantown. He also held lots from the original Oxmantown land grant and a lot on the north-side of St Stephen's Green. Richard Tighe (the younger) was successively MP for Belturbet 1703–13, Newtown(ards) 1715–27 and Augher 1727–36. He was also a member of the Irish Privy Council, Sheriff of Dublin in 1716 and he was an early member of the Dublin Society from 1731.[16] He married Barbara Bor of Drinagh, Co. Wexford and in 1715 he bought a house in Dawson Street from Bishop Peter Browne, where he had Bishop Charles Carr, former rector of St Paul's, as a neighbour. A Mrs Tighe was still recorded as living at No. 4 Dawson Street in 1798.[17]

Swift knew, and had an intense dislike for, Richard Tighe or Dick Tighe as he called him. In August 1711 in the *Journal to Stella* he made a number of disparaging references viz. 'Tighe and I took no notice of each other:', 'Dick Tighe and I meet and never stir our hats', 'Tighe … has been seen … beating her (his wife) two or three times …' and 'he resolves to part with her and they went to Ireland in different coaches'.[18] In August 1725, it was Richard Tighe who reported Swift's close friend Dr Thomas Sheridan to the authorities for his inappropriately titled sermon 'Sufficient unto the day is the evil thereof' which Sheridan had the misfortune to deliver on 1 August the anniversary of the accession of the king.[19] From that point onward Swift inserted disparaging allusions to Tighe into his Irish political writings and poetry. While Swift's own partisanship in politics, particularly on the issue of the Whig Tory party conflict, and his capacity to carry a dispute for many years was well-known, his negative references to Tighe nevertheless provide some insight into aspects of Tighe's personality. Yet Tighe's involvement, for over 40 years, in the management of parish affairs, first in St Michan's and then in St Paul's, as a churchwarden, regular attender at vestry meetings and director of the watch, indicated, at the very least his commitment to an active and involved participation in local affairs, even if we cannot discern his personal motivation for such a long-term and involvement. A final incident somewhat amusingly illustrates the nature of Richard Tighe and also the close network of 18th-century Protestant Dublin. In 1724 Viscount Middleton (Alan Brodrick) and parishioner of St Paul's reported how he had acquired one of Swift's Drapiers letters – 'His excellency shewed it to me, and told me, it struck at the dependency of Ireland on the crown of Great Britain. I had not read it over, but had bought one of them from Mr Tighe in the Council chamber, who told me, he bought two in the Castle from a hawker'.[20] The image of a rich well-connected member of the establishment selling a cheap, and highly controversial, political pamphlet to an even richer member of the establishment seems at the very least somewhat incongruous.

William Hendrick In the 1720s William Hendrick was probably the most significant property developer in the Smithfield St Paul's area of Dublin. Despite the wealth of detail that has been discovered on his property development, parochial and civic activities, his date of birth, death and many other aspects of his personal family situation have not yet been established. Evidence in the Registry of Deeds suggests that William Hendrick was a minor in 1719 and therefore that he was still a young man during his very active period of civic, parochial and property development activities in the 1720s.[21] William Hendrick's name was noted for the first time at a vestry meeting in St Paul's parish on 23 February 1721.[22] He and Richard Tighe served as churchwardens for three years 1723–25. His most important involvement in the vestry of the parish of St Paul's however was as a director of the watch committee, a position that he held for eight years from 1722, and one that helped him to oversee the protection of his property investments and presumably to sustain his rental income in the area. Hendrick was a governor of the Blue Coat School in 1725 and 1726 and in this role he was listed in the minute book as Master of the Trinity Guild. During his time as governor Hendrick was involved in two property issues germane to his area of expertise viz. a committee, established in December 1725, to 'consider of the expense of finishing of the inside of the Chappell and making it fit for divine service.' and a committee to review and make recommendations on properties on King Street and Church Street that had been willed to the school by Charles Wallis. Jonathan Swift was a Governor of the school at this time and attended at least three of the meetings at which Hendrick was present.[23]

In addition to his property development activities William Hendrick was also involved in municipal affairs as a member of the commons of the city assembly. The *Dublin Journal* of 13–17 December 1726 reported his election to the 'common council of this city, by the right honourable lord mayor and court of aldermen, for the three ensuing years'. The same edition also noted that Hendrick had served for the three previous years.[24] Many of his involvements in the business of the city assembly seemed to have been driven by his expertise in property and related matters and involved issues such as land sales, auditor of the accounts and the refurbishment of Tholsel. In July 1725 Hendrick was paid £25 7s. 9d for the provision of twenty-two pieces of alder for the use of the city.[25] In 1728 Hendrick was nominated to participate on a committee to treat with and agree rates with the pavers in the city, when the assembly felt that their rate of 'two pence half-penny per yard' was excessive even though the city supplied the stone.[26]

As already noted, William Hendrick got into financial difficulties in the late 1720s and after 1730 his name did not appear as a signatory at a vestry meeting in St Paul's parish. In 1731 the debtors lists in the *Dublin Gazette* recorded that 'William Hendrick late of aron's-quay but last of hendrick street in the suburbs of the city of dublin merchant' was listed as a debtor prisoner under the Four Courts Marshalsea.[27] In 1733 the vestry minute book of the parish of St Paul recorded that Mr Allen was reimbursed the modest sum of 11s. for Mr Hendrick's Easter Cess to the parish in 1730.[28]

Hendrick's name in the entry of seatholders from 1716 is crossed out and replaced by a Mr Hugh Wilson, unfortunately the date of the amendment is not recorded.[29] It appears that he joined the army and in lease memorials in the 1730s he was variously described as 'grandson of John Hendrick late of the city of Dublin Gent. Deceased' and as an ensign and a lieutenant in the regiments of Molesworth, Hamilton and Blakeney.[30] He was however still involved in property transactions in Francis Street as late as 1742.[31] A deed from 1737 noted that he was due to marry a 'Mary Redman daughter of Philip Redman of the county or Armagh'.[32] However, as already stated, despite this wealth of detail on his business, civic and parish activities, we still have relatively little information on his personal life and no meaningful insight into his politics, world-view or lifestyle.

Ezekiel Burridge   Ezekiel Burridge was instituted as the first rector for the newly established parish of St Paul on 4 May 1698.[33] The first incumbent of nearby St Mary's parish was the Revd Peter Browne who was an important figure in the Irish enlightenment, a leading Tory on the Irish episcopal bench and who went on to become provost of Trinity College and afterwards bishop of Cork and Ross.[34] Burridge must therefore have been seen by church and political leaders of the time as a man who was worthy of being appointed to the high-profile position of rector in a newly established parish. Ezekiel Burridge was born in Cork in 1661 and he was educated in Trinity College, Dublin.[35] He was ordained in 1686 and, in his short career, he held a number of important middle-ranking posts in the Church of Ireland including chancellor of the diocese of Down and Connor in the 1690s, proctor for Down clergy at the Convocation of 1704 and vicar-general for Dublin from 1703. Burridge was also chaplain to the lord chancellor, John Methuen, in the 1690s. He was curate in Finglas from 1687 where his rector was Samuel Foley, one of the original 'virtuoso' member of the Dublin Philosophical Society and who later became bishop of Down and Connor (1694–5).[36] Foley's appointment as bishop was part of efforts by the reforming bishops in the church in the 1690s to root out abuses in the northern dioceses and Burridge's involvement would seem to align him with the reformers within the church. On 23 February 1703 Burridge married Frances Moore daughter of Col. Roger Moore MP for Mullingar in the 1692–3 and the 1695–99 parliaments. Their son Ezekiel was baptised on 3 August 1707, however, he was buried some eighteen months later on 27 February 1709.[37] Samuel Foley also married a daughter of Col. Moore.[38]

   Burridge was a close associate of William Molyneux and the Molyneux – Locke correspondence makes several references to his ecclesiastical and business affairs. In 1697 he published a political tract, in Latin, justifying the glorious revolution. This book went into three editions and was apparently well received in London.[39] In 1701 he published a Latin translation of Locke's

Essay on human understanding.[40] In 1708, a 24 page pamphlet entitled, *A short view of the present state of Ireland: with regard particularly to the difficultys … In holding of a parliament. Written in … 1700. By the Reverend Dr. Burridge*, was published in London.[41] There was a brief reference to Burridge in Dunton's *Dublin scuffle* of 1699. In this work Dunton, a London booksellers and author, retells the story of his efforts to enter the Dublin book auction business and how this led to a dispute with Patrick Campbell, a leading Dublin bookseller. In a section dealing with those who had either supported or hindered his activities in Dublin, Dunton lists Mr Burridge as one of 'many … worthy clergymen that were encouragers of my auction.'[42]

Burridge appears to have been assiduous in his duties as rector and his signature appears regularly on the vestry minutes and in the baptismal, funeral and wedding registers.[43] However, he died young at the age of 46. There is some confusion in the sources over the exact date of his death. According to Falkiner he died on Tuesday 4 August 1707,[44] Ware records that he died about 1705[45] and Nidditch claims a date of 2 December 1707.[46] Burridge signed his last vestry minute on Monday 14 April 1707.[47] His will, which is in the National Archives of Ireland, is dated 3 August 1707.[48] Both Leslie and the St Paul's parish register record that he was buried in St Paul's on 5 August 1707.[49] Burridge nominated Alan Brodrick (later Viscount Midleton), then speaker of the Irish House of Commons and a leading Whig, and William Conolly, also a Whig, and also later to be speaker, as his executors. Conolly and Brodrick were later to be bitter rivals for the position of 'chief undertaker' in the Irish parliament in the first years of the reign of George I.[50] These choices as executors, imply a level of personal and intimate contact with leading members of the Whig establishment. When combined with the content of his pamphlets, they would indicate that Burridge must be seen as a Whig member of the parish clergy. This was apparently an unusual stance for parish clergy at this time as evidenced by the Tory sentiment of the convocation held during the reign of Queen Anne. Perhaps Burridge's Whig party politics reflected that of his parishioners including Alan Brodrick, Richard Tighe and Bruen Worthington. Overall his politics would seem to have operated on two levels. He was a reformer of church practice and management through his involvement in the restructuring of the management of the diocese of Down and Connor, in conjunction with his mentor and brother-in-law Foley. Yet he was also associated with leaders of the Whigs whose agenda could not be said to favour the established church and whose ultimate aims included the full repeal of the Test Act, a proposition which was not acceptable to most Irish Whigs let alone high church Tories.

Charles Carr   Charles Carr was the first curate of the parish of St Paul and the second rector of the parish. His succession to the post of rector of St Paul's in 1707 resulted in protracted legal proceedings both in Dublin and London. This dispute was but one episode in the long-running conflict between Archbishop

King and the dean and chapter of Christ Church Cathedral and a part of his reform programme to improve standards and to exercise his full power of appointment of parish clergy. On 4 August 1707 the dean and chapter of Christ Church, acting perhaps with indecent haste, but also within their understanding of their right of nomination, granted to them in the act of 1696 that established the parish, nominated the Revd William Williamson as the new rector of St Paul's. In the meanwhile Archbishop King nominated Charles Carr for the vacant post. In 1708 the dean and chapter of Christ Church brought a case on this issue to the Irish Common Pleas and won. Archbishop King appealed to the Irish Queen's Bench and had the verdict overturned. In turn in 1712 the dean and chapter appealed to the Queen's Bench in England and lost. Finally in 1717 the Dean and Chapter appealed to the English House of Lords and again lost. Despite these dramatic high-profile events there was no record of this dispute in the minutes of the minute book of St Paul's parish for this period.[51]

Archbishop King confirmed Carr in his appointment as rector of St Paul's to hold alongside his Blue Coat School headmastership. However, once appointed rector of St Paul's Carr could not fulfill his Sunday obligations in the school and, on 7 May 1708, the governors of the school passed a motion that 'from henceforth the Chaplaine of this Hospitall doe preach every Sunday Morning and read prayers in the Hospitall chapell and in the afternoon cathechise the boys and read prayers and that for the future none of the boys be permitted to goe to the parish Church.'[52] However, the governors were forced to back down a few days later when they noted that: 'the order made on the 7th of this inst. Ordering the chaplain to preach every Sunday morning to read prayers and cathecise in the afternoon be respited until the law suit between him and the Chapter of Christ Church about St Paul's parish be determined provided it continue not above six months and in the mean time Mr Carr doe performe his duty as formerly'.[53] The governors sought an update from Carr in December 1708 but it was ten years before the dispute was settled and it was only with Carr's translation to the bishopric of Killaloe in 1716 that the school was able to have a full-time chaplain again. Despite his difficulties with the governors of the Blue Coat School Carr left a legacy of £100 to the school on his death in 1739.[54]

Charles Carr was born in Donore, Co. Kildare in 1672, was educated in Trinity College Dublin taking his BA in 1695. He married Mary Dawson sister of the leading Dublin property developer Joshua Dawson. The St Paul's register recorded that in May 1708, Boyle the son of Charles and Mary Carr was baptized, in November 1706 Mary their daughter was baptized and on in August 1709 another daughter Ann was baptized.[55] Carr was married a second time to Anne Keating of Narraghmore, Co. Kildare.[56] Bishop Carr died in 1739 and was buried in St Patrick's cathedral.[57] He was also, for a time chaplain to the House of Commons, and in this role he used one of the set piece occasions of the Protestant calendar, to publish *A sermon, preached before the house of Commons in St. Andrew's church, Jan. 1716.*[58] The lord justices of the time, Lords Gallway and Grafton, in a note on Carr's elevation commented that his promotion to bishop should proceed as soon as possible 'because nothing can be more grateful to the gentlemen of Ireland that to see the chaplain of the House of Commons who is so much their favourite so well provided for'. In another note, from Gallway and Grafton, Carr was proposed for the bishopric of Killaloe in the following terms 'Dr Charles Kerr Chaplain of the House of Commons, to be Bishop of Killaloe, who besides His General good Character in other respects, has distinguished himself by his zeal for the Protestant Succession and the present happy settlement, a qualification to which we thought it highly for His Majestys Service, that a particular regard should be shown at this time.'[59]

Carr was known to Swift and in a letter to Bishop Atterbury dated 18 April 1716 we get some insight to Swift's view of Carr's character when Swift stated that 'We have also outdone you in the business of Ben Hoadley, and have recommended to a Bishoprick one whom you would not allow a Curate in the smallest of your parishes.'[60] Even for Swift however Carr wasn't all bad as, in a later controversy over the non-residency of bishops in their dioceses, Swift made an approving reference to Carr in one of his poems 'So God bless the Church, and three of our Mitres'.[61] The three bishops referred to, which included Carr, were the only members of the episcopal bench who voted against the bill in the House of Lords. Swift's approval was based on these three being of the Irish interest as opposed to the English interest in the house of bishops.[62]

Carr seems to have had a sense of humour and to have had a cordial relationship with his brother-in-law, Joshua Dawson. Writing to Dawson from Donegal on 14 July 1704, Carr noted, 'Last night I got to the famous city of Raphoe. I hope all friends in the little city of Dublin are well.'[63] In 1731 he leased a site on the east side of the Dawson Street from Joshua Dawson. The residence, which later belonged to Lord Clanricarde, appears to have been a large mansion, with gardens, and it was described in *Pue's Occurrences* of November 1743 as 'the corner house, next the college in Dawson Street, neatly and fully furnished, wherein the Earl of Clanrickard lately dwelt, with a fine backside, with gravel walks, and a fountain, with a large coach-house and stables'.[64] In Brooking's map of 1728 the area was shown as built up, but no site detail is shown. However, the Rocque map of 1756 shows what appears to be a large building on the corner of Dawson Street and Nassau Street, where Morrison Chambers is located today.[65] This site was the location of the fashionable Morrison Hotel in the nineteenth century.

Duke Tyrrell   Duke Tyrrell, the third rector, continued the tradition of rectors of St Paul's having an allegiance to the Whig cause. Tyrrell, who was instituted as rector on 11 June 1716, was born in Meath *c*.1681 and like many Dublin clergy of this period he was educated by Mr Jones in Dublin and at Trinity College Dublin. Tyrrell died in 1722 at the early age of 41 and he was buried in St Paul's.[66] Like Carr's appointment as rector, Tyrrell's was controversial. The philosopher George Berkeley, and later bishop of Cloyne, was interested in securing the vacancy at St Paul's and he actively canvassed for the position and secured support from the prince of Wales. Surviving correspondence on the appointment gives insight into the charged, and highly party-political, nature of contemporary church politics in Ireland.[67] Writing from London in May 1716 Berkeley believed that his desire to secure the rectorship of St Paul's 'cannot fail of success' because of the support that he has received from the prince of Wales and Mr Secretary Stanhope. He further noted that 'the living is reckoned to be worth about a hundred a year, but I can put the greater value on it because it is consistent with my (Trinity College) Fellowship.' However, by 26 May Berkeley's hopes had been seriously dented and he asked his friend Percival to plead his case with the duke of Grafton and assure him that he (Berkeley) was 'well affected to his Majesty's Governement'. However, he recognised that 'I have some reason to think that my competitors have wronged my character on the other side of the water' and 'I cannot but be solicitous to have my character cleared to the Lords Justices and others there who are probably misled by the calumny of interested persons who are strangers to me'.[68] Percival acceded to the request but his efforts were in vain and Percival later heard from Charles Dering that 'the Lord Justices having made a strong representation against him, and they say one Tirrel is to have that living'.[69] One possible reason for the campaign against Berkeley was that he was perceived as a Jacobite, a perception that may have arisen because of his publication some years earlier of a highly theoretical espousal of the Anglican doctrine of passive obedience.[70]

There was no doubting Tyrrell's politics. On 14 May 1716 he wrote a long letter to Robert Molesworth denouncing his rival and seeking Molesworth's help in securing St Paul's. Tyrrell letter stated his belief that Molesworth has 'interest and weight enough to sink a representation grounded on misinformation and that representation of Mr Berkly's character as a Tory will have influence enough with the prince and induce his royal highness .. to recoil from what has been done in his favour'.[71] The fact that Tyrrell's letter to Molesworth was among the State Papers Ireland may indicate that Molesworth used it in government circles.[72] Ironically, nearly 20 years later after spending time in America and on his appointment to the bishopric of Cloyne, Berkeley was consecrated in Dublin in May 1734 in, of all places, St Paul's parish church with Charles Carr as one of the officiating bishops.[73] Shortly after his appointment to St Paul's Tyrrell preached two ideologically significant sermons which were published under the title *The established church vindicated'*.[74] In 1717 he published, *A sermon preached at the consecration of Bp. Ralph Lambert, Apr, 23, 1717*, and in 1719 he published his sermon for 23 October to the House of Commons in St Andrew's church.[75]

Conclusion

In the last decades of the 17th century and the early decades of the 18th century Dublin was a Protestant city. The aim of this book has been to reconstruct aspects of an early 18th-century Dublin Protestant community by describing the property development, parochial and civic activities of the local Protestant elite in the Smithfield area, and in the newly established parish of St Paul in the suburb of Oxmantown. The individuals within this local community knew one another intimately, they were connected by parochial, civic, business and family ties and they were involved, to a greater or lesser extent, in some of the major national events and in the minutia of the local events of their time.

The evolution of the urban morphology of the Smithfield area, from the initial letting of the building plots by the corporation in the 1660s, until the completion of the construction of the area nearly a century later is a story of continuous, albeit uneven, growth. This growth was managed by a number of actors. In the first instance Dublin corporation leased development land to property speculators. The corporation also provided a range of other services such as scavenging, street lighting, paving and piped water. However the final morphology of the area was largely determined by the actions of private land speculators, property developers, master builders and tradesmen, financiers and house owners and lessees. The initial plan seems to have been to develop a new high-status extramural residential suburb of the city. To that end some key components of urban infrastructure, as understood at that time were put in place. Early initiatives included the granting of the development lots in 1665, the land grant to the duke of Ormond, the laying out of the Bowling Green by alderman Tighe, the development of the Blue Coat School, the enquaying of the north bank of the river Liffey and the construction and or reconstruction of two bridges. These were followed by the construction of a parish church and graveyard, and the provision of civic services such as lighting, paving, water and local security.

However, despite its initial good start in attracting many leading members of the Dublin civic and business community to the area, the Smithfield St Paul's area did not, in the long term, become one of the city's high-status residential areas. Aristocratic residents, while present throughout the period under review, were never the dominant residential group and Ormond never built in the area. Nevertheless the area retained sufficient kudos for the earl of Bective (Thomas Taylor) to build a Richard Castle designed house as late as 1738 on the western side of Smithfield and in the 1740s Sir Robert Echlin refurbished a large house in Queen Street. The archaeological evidence elicited from the excavations of plots 1–24 of the original 1665 allocation have already provided and will continue to provide a further corpus of hard evidence for the occupational evolution of the area. The analysis of the complex business practices of William Hendrick, the leading local property developer in the area in this period, in his lease terms, rental levels, payment terms, mortgage terms and the building conditions imposed on and by him provide significant insights into the workings of the Dublin building and rental sectors at this time.[1] While Hendrick's property development business failed in the late 1720s the development of the Smithfield St Paul's area continued apace. The ultimate failure of the Smithfield St Paul's area to develop into a high-status area can be traced to a number of factors. These included physical and environmental factors such as the location of the Royal Barracks and also the presence of industrial facilities, hay and cattle markets and a large number of taverns in the area. The lack of major aristocratic anchor tenant was also a negative factor. A change in the aesthetic taste of the urban middle-class, towards single-use areas was also emerging at this time. The deciding factor may have been the construction of Henrietta Street in the 1730s and the construction of Kildare House near St Stephen's Green by the earl of Kildare in the 1740s.

The analysis of the 237 pages of the vestry minute book of St Paul's parish has provided an insight into the workings of a major local civic institution in early 18th-century Dublin. This archive records the activities of hundreds of individuals who, with the exception of their inclusion in parish registers would, in most cases, be otherwise unknown to us today. The case for the publication of these important records of local civic life is demonstrated by the insights that they provide into many aspects of the working of this important local institution. While the parish vestry was a means of securing local participation in local affairs it also had the inherent danger of becoming controlled by a self-selecting group and even of becoming oligarchic. This structure also had the potential to become an agent of the central authorities and the imposition of ever greater civic responsibilities on the parish vestry could be seen as an indication that the central authorities felt that that the vestry could fulfill such a role. However, the essentially voluntary nature of the management structures with the activists drawn from the limited pool of adherents to the state religion (even though there was an element of compulsion in that those called to serve as parish officers were obliged to serve or to find a deputy) militated against the long-term success of such a strategy. Over time the demand for a broader and more complex range of local services such as security, water, lighting, cleaning, paving and the provision of poor relief, in an expanding and increasingly sophisticated city, required the employment of full-time staff. This in turn generated a requirement for a competent and full-time bureaucracy to oversee this increasingly complex organisational form. The minute book shows that the vestry of St Paul's parish made strenuous efforts to meet these demands, in a professional and competent manner. However the provision of such services also required significant revenue and the parish structure was not a suitable instrument for the raising of large sums of local taxation.

The minute book shows that the vestry meetings of the parish of St Paul were dominated by three themes – the management of the church property and facilities, the election of parish officers and the management of the increasingly intrusive burden of civic responsibilities imposed on the parish vestry. The vestry was also greatly exercised by the allocation of and sale of pews in church and this issue resulted in at least one situation where legal advice was required. The minute book has also provided direct evidence of the burden involved in carrying out these ecclesiastic and civic duties. The small number of signatures inscribed in parish vestry minute books in this period was, in all likelihood, an accurate reflection of the actual attendance at these meetings. The parish officers of St Paul's were aware of the formal roles that they occupied in the civic life of the city. The incidents recorded in the minute book, show that the vestry and its officers made strenuous efforts to fulfill their designated role in a competent manner, while spreading the burden of office across the available pool of qualifying parishioners. The formality inherent in the writing of minutes, and the preservation of the minute book itself, allowed the parish to retain written evidence of the actions of the parish officers in key matters such as appointments and financial stewardship. However, over time, it became increasingly difficult to expect these small groups of part-time volunteers drawn from the small pool of the local Protestant elite, to manage, in a professional and competent manner, the increasing burdens placed on them by legislation.

The minute book of St Paul's parish recorded in great detail the management of the parish watch. In fulfilling this role the parish had to nominate directors of the watch, constables and watchmen. There appears to have been no particular problem in finding members of the local elite to serve and as directors or local men to serve as watchmen. The elite had property interests to protect, as evidenced by the willingness of William Hendrick to finance the construction of a watch house from his own resources in the mid-1720s, and the watchmen could earn a modest income from their service. However there is evidence that the role of constable was unpopular and hard to fill, and there were numerous incidents where the parish nominee was rejected by the lord mayor. The paving returns reveal another important aspect of the workings of the local administrative bureaucracy. The lists themselves also provide important morphological and social information on the area. For example they provide some evidence for the continuation of high-status residents in the area until at least the mid-1740s.

The biographies of four leading vestrymen and the first three rectors of the parish have given further insight into the personalities, business affairs and the close interconnections of the local elite. From these biographies we can see aspects of their politics, business affairs and some details of their family life as recorded in the lifecycle of baptism, marriage, their children's baptisms and funerals. This elite had extensive connections throughout the city and the rest of the country and indeed further afield in London. The parishioners of St Paul appears to have been staunchly Whig in their politics as were the first three rectors of the parish. Again these biographies highlight the need for further research into individual biographies of local elites and even to develop prosopographies of vestrymen and parish officers in eighteenth-century Dublin.

The analysis in this book of the physical development of and the ecclesiastical and civic management of the Smithfield St Paul's area of Dublin in the first half of the eighteenth century has provided a case study of many aspects of the physical and institutional development of the city as a whole. Contemporary records regularly refer to the rapid growth of the north-side of the city — it was the place to be — a place of opportunity. From the initial 'greenfield' development in the 1660s through to William Hendrick's ambitious property ventures in the 1720s the Smithfield St Paul's area grew rapidly and the evidence from the lease agreements of William Hendrick give important insights into the property market in this period. Nevertheless Smithfield failed to become one of the premier high-status residential areas of the city. The vestry minutes of the parish of St Paul, led by a relatively small number of the Protestant local elite and drawn primarily from the merchant and administrative community, have left us a picture of the day-to-day actions of this important local institution as it sough to manage the increasingly complex responsibilities delegated to it by both national and local authorities. This book considers the actions of the local and civic elite of only one parish, there is ample scope for comparative work with the actions, composition and financing arrangements not only of other Dublin city parishes but also comparisons with those of other urban centres and with rural parishes in this period. The publication of vestry minute books for a number of Dublin parishes provides important primary sources for this comparative work.

By 1730 William Hendrick had lost his property business, by mid-century the Smithfield St Paul's area no longer had any pretensions of becoming a major high-status residential suburb. By the end of the 18th century the Protestant elite, outnumbered by the rising Roman Catholic population and the Roman Catholic merchant class, were loosing their control of the civic and business life of Dublin. Finally, in the early decades of the 19th century, the local Church of Ireland parish vestry became, perhaps what it should have been all along, a voluntary local group managing the fabric and finances of a religious institution – albeit one that retained a privileged position because of its role as the state church. But this future was not known by Burridge, Carr, Hendrick, Tighe, Tyrell, Westenra and Worthington and the others members of the local Protestant elite when they lived in the area. They sought to maintain the Protestant interest in Ireland, to manage the civic affairs of their neighbourhood as they saw fit and to build and maintain their businesses in a city, where, in the first half of the 18th century, they may have been the majority community but in a country where they were a minority. When assessing their lives and actions we should, as Sean Connolly has written, 'look at the Protestant elite primarily in its own terms: to reconstruct the way in which its members saw the society in which they lived the issues that seemed to them to matter most'.[2] This book has attempted to make a modest contribution to such a reconstruction in the context of one such Protestant elite in the confined space and time of the Smithfield St Paul's area of northern suburbs Dublin in the period 1698–1750.

Notes

Dates are according to the Julian or old style calendar for the day and month and according to the Gregorian calendar or new style for the year. Quotations from original sources retain the original spelling and word order; however, some punctuation marks (such as the insertion of full stops) have been silently added.

INTRODUCTION

1 For a explanation of the origin and usage of the term Protestant Ascendancy see: W.J. McCormack, *The Dublin paper war of 1786–1788, a bibliographical and critical inquiry including an account of protestant ascendancy and its 'baptism' in 1792* (Dublin, 1993) also J. Kelly, 'Conservative protestant political thought in late eighteenth-century Ireland' in S.J. Connolly (ed.), *Political ideas in eighteenth-century Ireland* (Dublin, 2000), pp 185–220 and T.C. Barnard, 'The Protestant interest, 1641–1660' in J.H. Ohlmeyer (ed.), *Ireland from independence to occupation* (Cambridge, 1995). Throughout this book I have used the term Protestant (upper case P), and infrequently the term conformist, when referring to the adherents of the state religion – the Church of Ireland. I have normally used the term catholic to refer to the majority population of Ireland and the term Roman Catholic when referring to that church as an institution or to specific individuals.

2 See D. Hayton, 'The development and limitations of protestant ascendancy: the Church of Ireland laity and public life, c.1660–1740', in R. Gillespie and W.G. Neely (eds), *The laity and the Church of Ireland, 1000–2000: all sorts and conditions* (Dublin, 2002), pp 104–32 for a full discussion on the nature of Protestant involvement in local and national administration in the eighteenth century.

3 S.J. Connolly, *Religion, law and power, the making of Protestant Ireland, 1660–1760* (Oxford, 2002), pp 2 and 104.

4 Jacqueline Hill, *From patriots to unionists: Dublin civic politics and Irish protestant patriotism, 1660–1840* (Oxford, 1997) p. 26.

5 The names of freemen have been catalogued by Gertrude Thrift – see Dublin City Archives: Gertrude Thrift (ed.), Dublin City Assembly Freedom Rolls R/1/05/08.

6 All of the members of this local Protestant elite were men. The participation of women in public office was almost non-existent at this time, although women do feature regularly in wills, in deeds and in a number of businesses such as printing and bookselling, see M. Pollard, *A dictionary of the members of the Dublin book trade 1550–1800 based on the records of the guild of St. Luke the evangelist Dublin* (London, 2000).

7 St Paul's Dublin Minute Book, Representative Church Body Library [RCB] P/273/6.1.

8 St Paul's Dublin Minute Book, RCB P/273/6.1, St Paul's Dublin Registers, RCB P/273/1.1 & 1.2, Registry of Deeds. King's Hospital, Ms 1 Account book and King's Hospital Ms 2 Board Minutes, File of 13 documents containing an original estimate, final invoice and various tradesmen's invoices for work carried out on Sir Robert Echlin's house in Queen Street – authors personal collection.

9 E. Synge, *The Synge letters: bishop Edward Synge to his daughter Alicia, Roscommon to Dublin 1746–1752*, ed. M.-L. Legg (Dublin, 1996) and 'Autobiography of Pole Cosby, of Stradbally, Queen's County, 1703–37', *Journal of the County Kildare Archaeological Society*, 5 (1906), pp 79–99, 165–84, 253–73, 311–24, 423–36.

10 Two unpublished theses have analysed specific aspects of Dublin in this period which are germane to the issues discussed in this book. Nuala Burke has described the evolution of the morphology of Dublin in this period including analyzing aspects of the property development activities of William Hendrick in the Smithfield St Paul's area. Rowena Dudley has reviewed the role of Church of Ireland parishes in the civic administration of Dublin in the eighteenth century. See N. Burke, 'Dublin, 1600–1800: a study in urban morphogenesis' (PhD thesis, TCD, 1972), R. Dudley, 'Dublin's parishes 1660–1729: the Church of Ireland parishes and their role in the civic administration of the city (PhD thesis, TCD, 1995). Also see R. Dudley, 'The Dublin parishes and the poor: 1660–1740', in *Archivum Hibernicum*, 53, (1999), pp 80–94 and J. Crawford and R. Gillespie, 'The Church of Ireland and its history: some recent writing' in *Search*, 27:1 (2004) for further sources on parish histories of the Church of Ireland in this period and T.C. Barnard, *Making the grand figure: lives and possessions in Ireland, 1641–1770* (New Haven and London, 2004).

1. THE CONSTRUCTION OF THE
SMITHFIELD ST PAUL'S AREA

1 See J. Summerson, *Georgian London* (Yale, 2003) for a now somewhat dated hypothesis of the early eighteenth-century urban development process and E. McKellar, *The birth of modern London: the development and design of the city 1610–1720* (Manchester, 1999) for a critique of Summerson's ideas and, for a more challenging hypothesis of the early modern urban development process. In 1962 the ESB asked Summerson to advise them on their proposed development of in Fitzwilliam Street where he described the street as 'one damned house after another … rubbish' *Bulletin of the Irish Georgian Society*, 5. (1962), p. 1.

2 Some aspects of the mortgage market are discussed later in this chapter . Insurance rates were set at 2.5 per cent for brick houses and 5 percent for timber houses – see R. Dudley, 'Fire insurance in Dublin, 1700–1860' in *Irish Economic and Social History*, 30, (2003), pp 24–51.

3 Hill, *From patriots to unionists*, pp 60–2 and pp 65–6. The records of the decisions of the city assembly were edited by John Gilbert and Lady Gilbert and published in nineteen volumes between 1889 and 1944. Since then these calendars have been used by countless

historians and they form the basis of much of our current understanding of the development of local government in Dublin over many centuries. The assembly meetings could consider from ten to twenty petitions, reports or resolutions at each session and it was often necessary to extend the meetings to deal with all the matters on the agenda. This extension was granted usually using the following formula 'Certain of the commons praying to enlarge the assembly till nine o'clock: ordered that the assembly be enlarged till nine o'clock' – example from 8 September 1724 – *Cal. An. Rec. Dub.*, vii, p. 278.

4 See N. Burke, 'Dublin 1600–1800' for a detailed analysis of this land grant and R. Dudley, 'St Stephen's Green: the early years 1664–1730' in *Dublin Historical Record*, 53, (2000), pp 157–79.

5 2 Geo.I ch.10 (Ire).

6 For a description of the city boundary see *Cal. An. Rec. Dub.*, i, pp 190–8, and xi, pp 489–91 and L. Barrow, '"Riding the franchises": The franchises of Dublin', *Dublin Historical Record*, 34 (1979–80), pp 135–8: and 36 (1982–3), pp 68–80.

7 See Burke, 'Dublin 1600–1800' for a discussion of the comparative social status of the Oxmantown and St. Stephen's Green grantees.

8 National Archives of Ireland D26295 indenture between Welbore Ellis and Samuel Byron 8 September 1744.

9 See P. Pearson, *The heart of Dublin: resurgence of an historic city* (Dublin, 2000), pp 378–92 for an overview of the occupational history of the Smithfield area also see Jacinta Prunty, *Dublin slums, 1800–1925: a study in urban geography* (Dublin, 1998) for descriptions of housing in the area in the nineteenth century.

10 See L.M. McCarthy, 'Evolution, present condition and future potential of the Smithfield area of Dublin' in *Irish Geography*, 24:2 (1990), pp 90–106 and G. Doran, 'Smithfield market past and present' in *Dublin Historical Record*, 50:2 (1997), pp 105–18 and the web site of the Historic Area Rejuvenation Project (HARP) at http://www.dublincity.ie /planning/harp2.html (20 January 2005).

11 *Cal. An. Rec. Dub.*, iv pp 382–3.

12 *Cal. An. Rec. Dub.*, v pp 285–6.

13 *Cal. An. Rec. Dub.*, iv pp 285–7.

14 John Dunton, *The Dublin scuffle* ed. A. Carpenter. (Dublin, 2000), p. 209 and John Dunton, *Teague land or a merry ramble to the wild Irish* (1698), ed. A. Carpenter (Dublin, 2003), p. 143.

15 Rawdon to Conway, *Cal. S.P., Ire., 1663–1665*, pp 589 and 591.

16 Rocque produced a number of versions of his maps of Dublin city and county, see P. Ferguson, *The A to Z of Georgian Dublin: John Rocque's maps of the city in 1756 and the county in 1760* (Kent, 1998) pp 5–6 which lists the Bowling Green although it is nearly surrounded by buildings. The version of the Rocque map included in Walter Harris' *The history of the antiquities of the city of Dublin* (Dublin, 1766, reprint Ballynahinch, 1994) does not name the same space as the Bowling Green.

17 *Cal. An. Rec. Dub.*, v pp 237–8 and J.W. deCourcy, 'The Liffey banks in Dublin, the early works of private developers' in *Dublin Historical Record*, 57:2 (Autumn 2004), pp 146–51.

18 Franc Myles, Archaeological Survey Smith-field, Margaret Gowan and Co. unpublished draft as of July 2004.

19 *Cal. An. Rec. Dub.*, vii, 415–6.

20 See William Duncan Map 1821 and Ordnance Survey map 1876 – *National Library of Ireland Historic Documents, Historic Dublin maps* (Dublin, nd).

21 These plots occupied the western side of Smithfield and the eastern side of Queen Street. Franc Myles, Archaeological Survey Smithfield, Margaret Gowan and Co. draft as of mid 2004. This section is heavily indebted to information provided by Frank Myles in an unpublished draft of the excavation report.

22 King's Hospital, Ms 1 Account book.

23 The location of Odacio Formica's glasshouse in Haymarket has recently been identified – see N. Roche, 'The glazing fraternity in Ireland in the seventeenth and eighteenth centuries' in *Bulletin of the Irish Georgian Society* 38, (1996–97), pp 66–94.

24 L. Clare, 'The Putland family of Dublin and Bray' in *Dublin Historical Record*, 54:1 (Spring 2001), pp 183–209.

25 P. Fagan, *The second city: portrait of Dublin, 1700–1760* (Dublin, 1986), p. 251 quoting an obituary from *Whalley's Newsletter*, 11 July 1720.

26 Walter Harris, *The history of the antiquities of the city of Dublin* (Dublin, 1766, reprint Bally-nahinch, 1994), records that John Hendrick was one of the city sheriffs in 1703 and that the same office was held by an R. Hendrick in 1707 and a Charles Hendrick in 1718.

27 Sir B. Burke, L.G. Pine (ed.), *Burke's A genealogical and heraldic dictionary of the landed gentry of Ireland* (4th edition, London, 1958), pp 767–8 and Lieut.-Colonel R.T. Wolfe, *The Wolfes of Forenaughts* (2nd edition, Guildford, nd), pp 43–7.

28 P. Roebuck, 'The Irish Registry of Deeds: a comparative study' in *Irish Historical Studies*, xviii, (1972–73), pp. 65–6.

29 National Archives of Ireland, D/16288, John Ellis to William Hendrick

30 *Dublin Gazette*, 14 March 1710.

31 National Archives of Ireland D/16290 indenture between William Hendrick of Dublin Merchant and Richard Hoffman esq. 7 January 1725.

32 National Archives of Ireland, D/16288 John Ellis to William Hendrick.

33 *Cal. An. Rec. Dub.*, vii, pp 248–9.

34 Slips were mooring points on the riverbank that were not dependent on the tide. De Courcy claims that the Gravel Walk Slip was enclosed and filled in 1811 – see J.W. de Courcy, *The Liffey in Dublin* (Dublin, 1996), p. 180.

35 *Cal. An. Rec. Dub.*, vii, pp 273–5.

36 Registry of Deeds 49/487/32952.

37 C.T. McCready, *Dublin street names, dated and explained* (Blackrock, 1987), p. 49 claims that it was named after Richard and Charles Hendrick.

38 Registry of Deeds, 6/248/28520.

39 National Archives of Ireland D/16291 lease from Mary Palliser to William Hendrick and D/16293 lease from Mary Palliser to John Murphy.

40 E. McKellar, *The birth of modern London: the development and design of the city 1660–1720* (Manchester, 1999), p. 65

41 Jonathan Swift, 'The truth of some maxims in state and government examined with reference to Ireland' in T. Scott (ed.), *The prose works of Jonathan Swift, D.D.*, vii (London, 1905), pp 63–72.

42 National Archives of Ireland D/16290 indenture between William Hendrick of Dublin Merchant and Richard Hoffman esq. 7 January 1725.

43 File of 13 documents containing an original estimate, final invoice and various tradesmen's invoices for work carried out on Sir Robert Echlin's house in Queen Street – authors personal collection.

44 *Dublin Gazette* 562, 5 Sept 1710

45 St Paul's Dublin Minute Book, RCB P/273/6.1, pp 189–210.

46 See T.C. Barnard, *Making the grand figure*, pp 282–309 for a detailed discussion on the demand for housing in Dublin in this period and for detail of the prices sought and achieved by rentiers in various parts of the city.

47 Pole Cosby, 'Autobiography of Pole Cosby of Stradbally, Queen's County, 1703–1737', in *Journal of the Kildare Archaeological Society and surrounding districts*, 5 (1906–8), pp 172, 256 and 435 and St Paul's Dublin Register, RCB P/273/1.2 p.16.

48 Registry of Deeds 9/44/3189 – will of John Hendrick.

49 Registry of Deeds 24/37/12957 dated 8 April 1719.
50 Registry of Deeds, 38/354/24570.
51 8 Geo I ch xiii (Ire.) and 5 Geo II ch vii (Ire).
52 *Burke's landed gentry of Ireland* (4th edition, London, 1958), p. 129.
53 Registry of Deeds, 46/189/28261 dated 5 March 1724.
54 This street was called Barrack Street and Tighe Street in contemporary documents. It was renamed Benburb Street in 1889 by Dublin Corporation as part of a long-term process whereby the renaming of streets and bridges in the city reflected the Unionist / Nationalist tension in Dublin Corporation in the nineteenth and early twentieth centuries. For a full overview of this issue see Y. Whelan, 'Naming Dublin: imperial power, nationalist resistance' in *Reinventing modern Dublin, streetscape, iconography and politics of identity* (Dublin, 2003), pp 94–111 and C. T., McCready *Dublin street names*, p. 134.
55 Registry of Deeds, 49/530/33166 dated 11 November 1726.
56 Registry of Deeds, 54/19/34709 dated 10 May 1727.
57 Registry of Deeds 106/88/72849.
58 Registry of Deeds, 68/127/47299. O'Brien describes James Swift as one of the leading Dublin bankers of the day – George O'Brien, *The economic history of Ireland in the eighteenth century* (Dublin, 1918), p. 354.
59 Registry of Deeds 106/88/72849.
60 Registry of Deeds 77/438/54281.
61 *Dublin Gazette*, 21 October 1710.
62 The issues that must inevitably have arisen from the presence of a major military facility in the parish have not been addressed in this book. An indicator of just one such impact is the regular appearance in the Dublin press of advertisements offering rewards for the return of deserters from various regiments stationed in the barracks.
63. R. Lee Cole, *The Wesley's came to Dublin* (London, 1947), pp 11, 21, 23 & 24.
64. David Wolley (ed.), *The correspondence of Johnathan Swift, D.D.* (four vols. Frankfurt, 1999–2005), iii, pp 98 & 127 and F. Elrington Ball (ed.), *The correspondence of Jonathan Swift, D.D.* (six vols, London, 1910–14), iii, p. 458 and Leslie pp 70 & 1146.
65. *Cal. An Rec. Dub.* viii. p. 135.
66. See Elizabeth Malcolm, *A history of St Patrick's Hospital, Dublin 1746–1989* (Dublin, 1989), pp 21–31 for a full discussion of the establishment of the committee of trustees, the acquisition of the site and the early finances of the project.

2. THE VESTRY OF ST PAUL'S PARISH – 1698–1750

1 Richard Burns, *The ecclesiastical law* (9th ed. 4 vols. London, 1842), p. 415.
2 For recent work on aspects of these topics see the as yet unpublished papers which were delivered at a conference on The Parish in Medieval and Early Modern Ireland held by the Group for the Study of Irish Historic Settlement in February 2003 – T.C. Barnard, 'The parish in eighteenth-century Ireland' and R. Gillespie, 'Urban parishes in reformed Ireland, the case of Dublin'. Also see R. Gillespie, 'Religion and urban society: the case of early modern Dublin' in P. Clarke and R. Gillespie (eds.) *Two capitals, London and Dublin, 1540–1840* (Oxford, 2001), pp 223–38 and J.P. Donohoe, 'The church of Ireland parishes of Lucan and Leixlip in the nineteenth century' (M Lit thesis, NUI Maynooth, 2003). Also see the introductions to two recent printed editions of parish vestry books which describe comparable events in two other city parishes viz. R. Gillespie (ed.), *The vestry record of the parish of St. John the Evangelist Dublin 1595–1658* (Dublin, 2002) and R. Gillespie (ed.) *The vestry record of the parish of St Catherine and St James Dublin, 1657–1692* (Dublin, 2004).
3 The vestry minute book, measures approximately 430mm by 310mm, is bound in leather and runs to 237 handwritten pages of meeting minutes and transcriptions of other documents. It also contains a number of extraneous manuscript and printed items inserted at various places in the book. It is hoped that this volume, edited by the present author, will be published in 2006 in the RCB's vestry minute book series.
4 9 Will. III, ch. 16 (Ire.).
5 Sir F.R. Falkiner, *The foundation of the hospital and free school of King Charles II, Oxmanstown, Dublin, commonly called the Blue Coat School* (Dublin, 1906), p. 126 and St Paul's Dublin Minute Book, RCB P/273/6.1 p. 5.
6 St Paul's Dublin Minute Book RCB P/273/6.1 pp 1–10.
7 Ibid., p. 10.
8 McParland, using Cork as his example, offers one possible explanation for the phenomenon of the construction of modest parish churches by the Church of Ireland when he commented that 'If the rebuilding of most of the churches in Cork city after the siege was to be funded from a coal tax, it was only discreet (in a city where two-thirds of the population was Roman catholic) that these churches be dignified but not too showy.' E. McParland, *Public architecture in*

Notes

61

Ireland 1680–1760 (New Haven, 2001), pp 48–9. The nineteenth-century church of St. Paul's was closed in the 1980s and now operates as a local enterprise centre.

9 Elmes does not list any images for St Paul's – see R.M. Elmes and M. Hewson, Catalogue of Irish topographical prints and original drawings (Dublin, 1975 revised and expanded edition) and Andrew Bonar Law of the Neptune Gallery (December 2004) has not discovered any image of the first St Paul's church see Andrew Bonar Law and Charlotte Bonar Law, A contribution towards a catalogue of the prints and maps of Dublin city and county (2 vols, Dublin, 2005).

10 G.N. Wright, Historical guide to ancient and modern Dublin (London, 1821), pp 165–7.

11 St Paul's Dublin Minute Book RCB P/273/6.1 pp 2 & 19.

12 Ibid., p 49

13 Cal. An. Rec. Dub., v. vii pp 98–100, and St Paul's Dublin Minute Book, RCB P/273/6.1 p 49

14 St Paul's Dublin Minute Book RCB P/273/6.1 pp 6–10.

15 Alan Broderick, later Lord Middleton, leader of the Whig party in the Irish House of commons at this time was not a very active member of the parish – see E.M. Johnston-Liik, History of the Irish parliament, 1692–1800. (six vols Belfast, 2002) for biographical detail.

16 See E. Sheridan, 'Living in the capital city, Dublin in the eighteenth century' in Joseph Brady and Anngret Simms (eds.), Dublin through space and time (Dublin, 2001), pp 135–65 for a full description of the social profile of Dublin at the end of the eighteenth century.

17 Sarah Sharples was the widow of William Sharp the first sexton of the parish – the use of varying forms of spelling for surnames was not uncommon in this period, even within a single document. St Paul's Dublin Minute Book, RCB P/273/6.1 pp 3 & 28.

18 In the early years of the twentieth century the Parish Register Society of Dublin published a number of parish registers and in recent years the RCB has reissued some of the earlier publications and published some further registers and also some vestry minute books. These publications have given scholars easier access to these important primary sources and are helping to create a deeper understanding of the day-to-day activities of and impact of the parish vestries and of parish officers in eighteenth-century Ireland.

19 See S. Wright (ed.), Parish, church and people, local studies in lay religion (London, 1988) for a discussion on the role of the parish vestry in England.

20 R. Gillespie (ed.), The vestry records of the parish of St. John the Evangelist, pp 1–10.

21 St Bride's Dublin Minute Book, RCB P/327/3.1 vol. I, 1662–1742 p. 108 memorandum 18 October 1683.

22 St Paul's Dublin Minute Book, RCB P/273/6.1 p 86.

23 12 Geo. I, ch. 9 (Ire.).

24 St Paul's Dublin Minute Book, RCB P/273/6.1 passim.

25 Ibid.

26 Dublin Gazette, 16 April 1730. This volume was printed twice in Dublin in the eighteenth century – Humphrey Prideaux, Directions for church-wardens for the faithful discharge of their office. (Dublin, 1726) and Directions for church-wardens for the faithful discharge of their office. (Dublin, 1756).

27 See T.C. Barnard, A new anatomy of Ireland, p. 242 for a discussion on this issue.

28 See St Paul's Dublin Minute Book, RCB P/273/6.1 pp 82–3 where a John Kenny is listed as on of the constables of the parish for 1731 and signed the minute of the meeting with his mark and p.13.

29 Most parish vestry minutes are a lot less informative that the minutes of the city assembly as recorded in the Calendar of the ancient records of Dublin which deal with somewhat similar issues and which were attended by, and recorded by, many of the same individuals as those who attended local parish vestry meetings. As with other parishes throughout this period many of the members of the vestry of St Paul's parish including William Hendrick, Henry Burrows, Richard Tighe and Joseph Kane were also members of the city assembly and they were also on the governing bodies of organization such as the Blue Coat School and later in the Dublin Society. As such they would have been familiar with the more detailed record keeping practices of these bodies.

30 St Paul's Dublin Minute Book, RCB P/273/6.1 p. 3.

31 Ibid., p. 13.

32 Ibid., p. 142.

33 Ibid., p. 28

34 Dublin City Archives, Monk Mason MS. Part III pp 151–2 quotes a figure of 364 spaces for 52 pews in St Paul's. Acheson has mentioned an estimated capacity of about 1,000 but this seems high in the context of the number of pews and the Monk Mason data. Acheson, A history of the Church of Ireland 1691–2001 (Dublin, 2nd ed., 2002), pp 50–2.

35 St Paul's Dublin Minute Book, RCB P/273/6.1 p. 9.

36 Ibid., p. 21.

37 Ibid., p. 84.

38 Dublin Gazette, 18 July 1710 and 5 Sept. 1710.

39 *Dublin Gazette*, 13 March 1711.
40 St Paul's Dublin Minute Book, RCB P/273/6.1 pp 44–5.
41 See Barnard, *A new anatomy of Ireland*, p. 239 for a discussion of the composition of the seat holders in parish churches.
42 8 Geo. I ch. 10 (Ire.) and B. Henry, *Dublin hanged: crime law enforcement and punishment in late eighteenth century Dublin* (Dublin, 1993), p. 14 and N. Garnham, 'Police and public order in eighteenth-century Dublin', in Clarke and R. Gillespie (eds.), *Two capitals*, pp 81–91.
43 St Paul's Dublin Minute Book, RCB P/273/6.1 p. 123.
44 See *Dublin Gazette*, 1 Dec.1711 for typical entries.
45 Cited in J. Brady, *Catholics and catholicism in the eighteenth century press* (Maynooth, 1965), pp 51 & 60. The convent in Channell Row seems to have been a regular focus of attention from the authorities as it was also raided shortly after its establishment in 1712 see *Dublin Gazette*, 9 Sept 1712.
46 St Paul's Dublin Minute Book, RCB P/273/6.1 p. 52.
47 Ibid., p 53.
48 Ibid., p. 62.
49 Paul Ferguson, *The A to Z of Georgian Dublin.*
50 St Paul's Dublin Minute Book, RCB P/273/6.1 p.92.
51 St Paul's Dublin Minute Book, RCB P/273/6.1 p. 73.
52 Ibid., p. 83.
53 Ibid., p. 93.
54 3 Geo. 2 ch xiii (Ire.).
55 *A proclamation by the right honorable lord mayor of the city of Dublin for the better amendement of the pavements and cleansing the streets of the city of Dublin* (Dublin, 1730).
56 St Paul's Dublin Minute Book, RCB P/273/6.1 p. 77.
57 For example in May 1731 William Hendrick was listed twice for Tighe Street – St Paul's Dublin Minute Book, RCB P/273/6.1 p. 84.
58 St Paul's Dublin Minute Book, RCB P/273/6.1 pp 84–5.
59 Ibid., p. 89.
60 Ibid., p. 103.
61 Ibiid., P/273/6 –Vestry accounts 1735 p. 115.
62 A cess book was listed in the inventory of parish assets of 1731 – St Paul's Dublin Minute Book, RCB P273/6.1 p. 87.
63 There was no expenditure recorded under this heading in the last two sets of accounts that I have analyses i.e. those for 1738 and 1739 and I am unaware at this time as to why this item no longer appeared in the churchwardens accounts as transcribed into the minute book.
64 Churchwardens Accounts St. Catherine's 1691 RCB P/117 5/1 p.357.

65 St Paul's Dublin Minute Book, RCB P/273/6.1 p. 48.
66 M. Pollard, *A dictionary of the members of the Dublin book trade 1550–1800 based on the records of the guild of St. Luke the evangelist Dublin* (London, 2000), pp 591–2, describes John Wattson as a bookseller, bookbinder and press corrector of figures who had a shop in Merchants' Quay. He started the series of *Watson's almanacs* that ran from 1727 (with the exception of 1728) until the 1840s and which constitutes a major source on the detail of addresses, businesses and individuals in eighteenth-century Dublin. Other book-binding clients of his included Marsh's Library in 1731.
67 St Paul's Dublin Minute Book, RCB P/273/6.1 p. 237
68 Registry of Deeds 64/352/44179 – recorded a rent of £40 per annum paid by Williamson to Hendrick in 1730.

3. THE LOCAL ELITE OF THE SMITHFIELD ST PAUL'S AREA

1 St Paul's Dublin Minute Book, RCB P/273/6.1 p. 52.
2 Ibid., pp 3 and 4.
3 Ibid., p.9.
4 Dublin City Archives: Gertrude Thrift (ed.), Dublin City Assembly Freedom Rolls R/1/05/08.
5 St Paul's Dublin Minute Book, RCB P/273/6.1.
6 Registry of Deeds, 1/1–5/1–3, 16/58/6893 and 8/314/2816.
7 P.B. Eustace (ed.), *Registry of deeds Dublin abstracts of wills, 1708–1745*, i (Dublin, 1956), p. 35.
8 National Archives Kew, State Papers Ireland SP/63/374. pp 290–3.
9 Carr Charles, *A sermon preach'd before the honourable House of Commons at St. Andrew's-Church, Dublin, January the 30th, 1715/16* (Dublin, 1716).
10 St Paul's Dublin Register, RCB P/273/1.1 pp 29 & 60.
11 *The registers of the church of St. Michan's Dublin, 1636–1700* (Dublin, 1909), p. 468.
12 St Paul's Dublin Minute Book, RCB P/273/6.1 p.5.
13 Ibid., p. 9.
14 Dublin City Archives, Monk Mason MS. Part III and St Paul's Dublin Register, RCB P/273/1.1.
15 *Irish Georgian Society records of eighteenth century domestic architecture and decoration in Dublin* (Dublin, 1913) v, pp 31–34 and see J. Wilding, 'The Tighes of Rossanagh' in

Ashford and District Historical Journal 2 (1992), 37–8 for more detail.

16 Johnston-Liik, *History of the Irish Parliament,* vi. p. 395 and F. Mulligan, *The founders of the Royal Dublin Society* (Dublin, 2005), p. 56.

17 *Irish Georgian Society records of eighteenth century domestic architecture and decoration in Dublin* (Dublin, 1912), iv pp 9, 102 and 110.

18 Jonathan Swift, *The journal to Stella* (London, 1897), pp 96, 176, 229 and 242.

19 For a fuller discussion of this issue and of Swift's other references to Tighe see I. Ehrenpreis, *Swift, the man, his works and the age* (3 vols, London, 1962–83), iii, pp 362–5, 578–9 and 830–1.

20 Ehrenpreis, *Swift, the man, his works and the age* iii, p. 252 citing William Coxe, *Memoirs of the life and administration of Sir Robert Walpole* (3 vols, London, 1798).

21 Registry of Deeds 23/153/12950.

22 St Paul's Dublin Minute Book, RCB P/273/6.1 p. 52.

23 King's Hospital Ms 2 Board Minutes, pp 284–5 and passim.

24 *Dublin Journal,* 17 December 1726.

25 *Cal. An. Rec. Dub.*, vii p. 305.

26 Ibid., vii pp 416–7.

27 *Dublin Gazette,* 7 December 1731 & 10 December 1731.

28 St Paul's Dublin Minute Book, RCB P/273/6.1 p. 100.

29 Ibid., p.45.

30 Registry of Deeds 53/38/34321, 77/438/54281, 101/32/69675 and 104/414/73684.

31 Registry of Deeds 104/414/73684.

32 Registry of Deeds 87/265/61566.

33 Canon J.B. Leslie and W.J.R. Wallace (ed.), *Clergy of Dublin and Glendalough biographical succession lists* (Dublin, 2001).

34 See A.R. Winnett, *Peter Browne, provost, bishop, metaphysician* (London, 1974).

35 George Dames Burtchaell and Thomas Ulick Sadlier, *Alumni Dublinenses.* (London, 1924).

36 Foley was Swift's bishop during his time as rector of Kilroot in the 1690s. See T.K. Hoppen, *The common scientist in the seventeenth century* (London, 1970) for further aspects of Foley's interests. Foley was a bibliophile and his library of several hundred volumes later became part of the extensive library of Archbishop William King much of which is now housed in the Bolton Library in Cashel. Two volumes from Ezekiel Burridge's library were also part of King's library see R.S. Matteson (ed.), *A large private park, the collection of archbishop William King 1650–1729* (Cambridge, 2003).

37 St Paul's Dublin Register, RCB P/273/1.1 pp 30 & 122.

38 Johnston-Liik, *History of the Irish Parliament,* v, pp 395–6.

39 Ezekiel Burridge, *Historia nuperae rerum mutationis in Anglia in qua res a Jacobo rege contra leges Anglia & Europae libertatem, & abordinibus Angliae contra regem patratae, duobos libris recentsentur* (London, 1697). There are at least three imprints from A. & J. Churchill, Sam Buckley, and Edward Castle and Sam Buckley. See Early English Books on-line (October 15 2004) http://wwwlib.umi.com.eebo/image?vod=6 1.htm and *The correspondence of John Locke,* ed. E. S. De Beer (Oxford, 8 vols, 1976–1989), vi, p. 8.

40 John Locke, *De intellectu humano in quatuor libris* (London, 1701).

41 Ezekiel Burridge, *A short view of the present state of Ireland: with regard particularly to the difficultys … In holding of a parliament. Written in … 1700. By the Reverend Dr. Burridge.* (London, 1708).

42 John Dunton, *The Dublin scuffle,* ed. A. Carpenter (Dublin, 2000), p. 98.

43 Register of St Paul's Parish Dublin, RCB Library, P/273/1.1 and St Paul's Dublin Minute Book, P/273/6.1 passim.

44 Falkiner, *The foundation of the Hospital and Free School*, pp 132–3.

45 See Sir J. Ware, *The whole works of Sir James Ware concerning Ireland, in three volumes,* (Dublin, 1745), ii p. 263 – this lack of certainty about an event that occurred only thirty-eight years previously, seems strange given that colleagues of Burridge were still active at this time.

46 P.H. Nidditch, 'Two notes on Burridge' in *The Locke Newsletter* (1973), pp 41–3.

47 St Paul's Dublin Minute Book, RCB P/273/6 P25.

48 CD Rom – *Irish Records Index Vol. 1, Index of Irish Wills 1484–1858, Records at the National Archives of Ireland,* (Dublin, ND). Citing National Archive reference Prerogative Will Book/F/223a Document ID:9659.

49 Leslie and Wallace (eds.), *Clergy of Dublin and Glendalough,* p. 445 and St Paul's Dublin Register, RCB P/273/1.1 p. 13.

50 See P. McNally, 'Wood's halfpence, Carteret and government of Ireland, 1723–6' in *Irish Historical Studies,* 30:119 (May 1997), pp 354–76.

51 These events are more fully described in Falkiner, *The foundation of the Hospital and Free School,* pp 132–3 and A. Acheson, *A history of the Church of Ireland 1691–2001* (Dublin, revised 2nd edition, 2002), pp 53–5 also for background see G.T. Stokes, *Some worthies of the Irish church* (London, 1900), pp 145–308.

52 King's Hospital, Ms. 2 Board Minutes, P 203.

53 Ibid., P 204.

54 King's Hospital, Ms 1 Account Book, P 535.

55 St Paul's Dublin Minute Book, RCB P/273/1.1.

56 Leslie and Wallace *Clergy of Dublin and Glendalough*, p. 466.

57 There is no listing of a monument to Carr in St Patrick's cathedral see V. Jackson, *The monuments in St Patrick's Cathedral Dublin* (Dublin, 1987).

58 C. Carr, *A sermon, preached before the House of Commons in St. Andrew's Church, Jan. 1716*, (Dublin, 1716)

59 The National Archives Kew, SP/63/374 pp 133 & 205.

60 Irwin Ehrenpreis, *Swift, the man, his works, and the Age, Volume III, Dean Swift* (London, 1983), iii, pp 172–3 and Jonathan Swift, *The correspondence of Jonathan Swift, Vol. II, Letters 1714–1726, nos. 3001–700*, ed. David Whoolley (Frankfurt am Main, 2001) p. 160.

61 Jonathan Swift, *The poems of Jonathan Swift*, ed. Harold Williams (3 vols, Oxford, 1937), iii, p. 805.

62 L.A. Landa, *Swift and the Church of Ireland* (Oxford, 1965), p. 122.

63 Quoted in James Anthony Froude, *The English in Ireland in the eighteenth century* (3 vols., London, 1872–4), i, pp 282–3, quoting Dawson Mss, Dublin Castle.

64 *Pue's Occurrences*, 26 Nov. 1743.

65 C. Brooking, *A map of the city and suburbs of Dublin* (London, 1728) and J. Rocque, *An exact survey of the city and suburbs of Dublin, 1756* (London, 1756).

66 Leslie and (eds.), *Clergy of Dublin and Glendalough*, p. 1131.

67 See D. Berman, 'The Jacobitism of Berkeley's Passive Obedience' in *Journal of the History of Ideas*, 48:2 (April-June 1986) p. 310 and S. Connolly, 'Reformers and High Fliers' in A.Ford, J. McGuire & K. Milne, *As by law established: the Church of Ireland since the reformation* (Dublin, 1995), pp 152–165.

68 G. Berkeley, *The works of George Berkeley*, ed. A.A. Luce and T.E. Jessop (London, 1948–57), viii, p. 99.

69 B. Rand, *Berkely and Percival* (Cambridge, 1914), p. 159.

70 George Berkeley, *The works*, vi, p. 15.

71 The National Archives, Kew, SP/63/374, nos. 185–88.

72 Also see Berman, 'Jacobitism of', p. 311.

73 A.A. Luce, *The life of George Berkeley bishop of Cloyne* (London, 1949), p. 159.

74 Duke Tyrrell, *The established church vindicated from the charges of schism: with an answer to the main arguments and principles of Doctor Hick's, and his followers: by which they endeavour to maintain the charge, in two sermons preach'd in the parish-church of St Paul's, Dublin. On the fourth and fifth of November, 1716* (Dublin, 1716).

75 Duke Tyrrell, *A sermon preached at the consecration of Bp. Ralph Lambert, Apr, 23, 1717*, (Dublin, 1717) and idem, *A sermon preach'd at St. Andrew's Dublin … October 23rd 1719 being the anniversary thanksgiving-day for the deliverance from the horrid rebellion which broke out … 23rd of October 1641*. (Dublin, 1719).

CONCLUSION

1 See McKellar, The birth of modern London, pp 57–61 for discussion of the issue of building leases in London in this period and its impact on the building sector.

2 S.J. Connolly, Religion, law and power: the making of protestant Ireland, 1660–1760 (Oxford, 2002), p. 4.